Sweet
Cravings

Jean Paré

companyscoming.com
visit our web-site

Front Cover

1. Instant Maple Walnut Fudge, page 42
2. Marshmallow Brownie Dreams, page 138
3. Tropical Rumba Cheesecake, page 68
4. Raspberry Turkish Jellies, page 30

Props Courtesy Of:
Anchor Hocking Canada
Cornell Trading Ltd.
La Cache
Pfaltzgraff Canada

Back Cover

1. Mango Raspberry Trifles, page 106
2. Lemon Poppy Loaf, page 24
3. Sticky Date Pudding, page 101
4. Pastry Triangles With Pears, page 86

Props Courtesy Of:
Cornell Trading Ltd.
La Cache

Sweet Cravings

Copyright © Company's Coming Publishing Limited
All rights reserved worldwide. No part of this book may be reproduced in any form by any means without written permission in advance from the publisher. Brief portions of this book may be reproduced for review purposes, provided credit is given to the source. Reviewers are invited to contact the publisher for additional information.

Fourth Printing March 2003

National Library of Canada Cataloguing in Publication

Paré, Jean
        Company's coming, sweet cravings / Jean Paré.

(Original series)
Includes index.
ISBN 1-895455-96-0

        1. Desserts. 2. Cake. 3. Pastry. I. Title. II. Series.

TX765.P37 2002   641.8'6   C2002-902712-8

Published by
COMPANY'S COMING PUBLISHING LIMITED
2311 - 96 Street
Edmonton, Alberta, Canada T6N 1G3
Tel: (780) 450-6223   Fax: (780) 450-1857
www.companyscoming.com

Company's Coming is a registered trademark owned by Company's Coming Publishing Limited

Printed in Canada

Visit us on-line

companyscoming.com

| Who We Are | Browse Cookbooks | Cooking Tonight? | Home |

everyday ingredients

feature recipes

feature recipes — Cooking tonight? Check out this month's *feature recipes*—absolutely FREE!

tips and tricks — Looking for some great kitchen helpers? *tips and tricks* are here to save the day!

reader circle — In search of answers to cooking or household questions? Do you have answers you'd like to share? Join the fun with *reader circle*, our on-line question and answer bulletin board. Great for swapping recipes too!

cooking links — Other interesting and informative web-sites are just a click away with *cooking links.*

cookbook search — Find cookbooks by title, description or food category using *cookbook search*.

contact us — We want to hear from you—*contact us* lets you offer suggestions for upcoming titles, or share your favourite recipes.

Company's Coming®

Canada's
most popular
cookbooks!

Company's Coming Cookbook Series

Quick & easy recipes, everyday ingredients!

Original Series

- Softcover, 160 pages
- 6" x 9" (15 cm x 23 cm) format
- Lay-flat binding
- Full colour photos
- Nutrition information

Greatest Hits Series

- Softcover, 106 & 124 pages
- 8" x 9 9/16" (20 cm x 24 cm) format
- Paperback binding
- Full colour photos
- Nutrition information

Lifestyle Series

- Softcover, 160 pages
- 8" x 10" (20 cm x 25 cm) format
- Paperback & spiral binding
- Full colour photos
- Nutrition information

Special Occasion Series

- Hardcover & softcover, 192 pages
- 8 1/2" x 11" (22 cm x 28 cm) format
- Durable sewn binding
- Full colour throughout
- Nutrition information

See page 157 for a complete listing of **all** cookbooks or visit companyscoming.com

Table of Contents

Beverages

Cakes

Desserts

Pies & Pastry

Squares

Measurement Tables

Cookbook List

The Company's Coming Story

Jean Paré grew up understanding that the combination of family, friends and home cooking is the essence of a good life. From her mother she learned to appreciate good cooking, while her father praised even her earliest attempts. When she left home she took with her many acquired family recipes, a love of cooking and an intriguing desire to read recipe books like novels!

"never share a recipe you wouldn't use yourself"

In 1963, when her four children had all reached school age, Jean volunteered to cater the 50th anniversary of the Vermilion School of Agriculture, now Lakeland College. Working out of her home, Jean prepared a dinner for over 1000 people which launched a flourishing catering operation that continued for over eighteen years. During that time she was provided with countless opportunities to test new ideas with immediate feedback—resulting in empty plates and contented customers! Whether preparing cocktail sandwiches for a house party or serving a hot meal for 1500 people, Jean Paré earned a reputation for good food, courteous service and reasonable prices.

"Why don't you write a cookbook?" Time and again, as requests for her recipes mounted, Jean was asked that question. Jean's response was to team up with her son, Grant Lovig, in the fall of 1980 to form Company's Coming Publishing Limited. April 14, 1981, marked the debut of "150 DELICIOUS SQUARES", the first Company's Coming cookbook in what soon would become Canada's most popular cookbook series.

Jean Paré's operation has grown steadily from the early days of working out of a spare bedroom in her home. Full-time staff includes marketing personnel located in major cities across Canada. Home Office is based in Edmonton, Alberta in a modern building constructed specially for the company.

Today the company distributes throughout Canada and the United States in addition to numerous overseas markets, all under the guidance of Jean's daughter, Gail Lovig. Best-sellers many times over in English, Company's Coming cookbooks have also been published in French and Spanish. Familiar and trusted in home kitchens around the world, Company's Coming cookbooks are offered in a variety of formats, including the original softcover series.

Jean Paré's approach to cooking has always called for quick and easy recipes using everyday ingredients. Even when travelling, she is constantly on the lookout for new ideas to share with her readers. At home, she can usually be found researching and writing recipes, or working in the company's test kitchen. Jean continues to gain new supporters by adhering to what she calls "the golden rule of cooking": never share a recipe you wouldn't use yourself. It's an approach that works— *millions of times over!*

Foreword

I love sweets! In fact, dessert is the course that I most look forward to. The most memorable meals I've ever had were those that were followed by just the right dessert. It's true that the last thing eaten is the first thing remembered.

And my love of sweets doesn't end with desserts. I also enjoy having a batch of squares on hand for friends who drop by or a dish of candied nuts on the coffee table to nibble during the game. On lazy weekend mornings, I love sticky buns, warm from the oven, drizzled with icing. And on chilly winter evenings, I enjoy a rich, frothy mug of hot chocolate. And then there are those times when I just feel like a little something to satisfy that sweet tooth craving!

My particular weakness is chocolate! There is something so irresistible about the smooth, creamy rich texture and taste of chocolate. It's the ultimate comfort food—equally at home in puddings and sauces, cakes and pies, and squares and pastries. Its versatility and popularity make it an ideal treat or dessert ingredient.

Many of us lead such busy lives that dessert is often the one course to be dropped from the menu when planning a meal. What a shame, when so many of us enjoy a sweet ending! But dessert preparation doesn't have to be time-consuming and labour intensive. *Sweet Cravings* has many simple recipes for desserts and treats that are quick and easy to prepare.

I have always thought that sweets are best enjoyed in the company of family and friends. But why not make a batch of something sweet and surprise your neighbour, your child's classmates or your

office colleagues? Let the kids help prepare the treat of their choice. Or have a friend or two drop by for an afternoon of candy making.

Sweet Cravings was fun to write—and even more fun to test! I know that many of these recipes will be prepared over and over again in your own home—and many a sweet craving will be satisfied!

Jean Paré

Each recipe has been analyzed using the most up-to-date version of the Canadian Nutrient File from Health Canada, which is based on the United States Department of Agriculture (USDA) Nutrient Data Base. If more than one ingredient is listed (such as "hard margarine or butter"), then the first ingredient is used in the analysis. Where an ingredient reads "sprinkle," "optional," or "for garnish," it is not included as part of the nutrition information.

Margaret Ng, B.Sc. (Hon), M.A.
Registered Dietitian

Fluffy Duck

A thick, creamy, sun-tinted beverage with a delicate orange flavour.
A perfect sipping beverage to be savoured slowly.

Crushed ice	2 tbsp.	30 mL
Advocaat liqueur	2 tbsp.	30 mL
White rum	1 tbsp.	15 mL
Orange-flavoured liqueur (such as Grand Marnier)	1 tbsp.	15 mL
Prepared orange juice	1/4 cup	60 mL
Half-and-half cream	1/4 cup	60 mL
Orange twist, for garnish	1	1
Maraschino cherries, for garnish	2	2

Put ice into 6 oz. (170 mL) glass. Pour next 5 ingredients over ice. Stir. Makes 3/4 cup (175 mL).

Garnish with orange twist and cherries. Serves 1.

1 serving: 467 Calories; 14.3 g Total Fat; 116 mg Sodium; 4 g Protein; 55 g Carbohydrate; trace Dietary Fibre

Pictured on page 17.

Mai Tai

A summer classic! The perfectly blended flavours of orange, pineapple and lime laced with rum! Close your eyes and imagine the sand, the surf and the palms without ever leaving home.

White (or amber) rum	1 oz.	30 mL
Dark rum	1 oz.	30 mL
Bitter orange-flavoured liqueur (such as Curaçao)	1/4 oz.	8 mL
Lime juice	2 tsp.	10 mL
Simple Cocktail Syrup, page 10	2 tsp.	10 mL
Crushed ice	1 cup	250 mL

(continued on next page)

Beverages

| Crushed ice | 3 tbsp. | 50 mL |
| Pineapple juice | 1/2 cup | 125 mL |

Combine first 6 ingredients in cocktail shaker or jar with tight-fitting lid. Shake well.

Strain through sieve over second amount of ice in 12 oz. (341 mL) glass. Discard crushed ice in shaker.

Stir in pineapple juice. Makes 1 cup (250 mL). Serves 1.

1 serving: 272 Calories; 0.1 g Total Fat; 3 mg Sodium; trace Protein; 31 g Carbohydrate; trace Dietary Fibre

Pictured on page 17.

─────────

Planter's Punch

Perfect for a hot summer afternoon. This rosy pink beverage is tart and refreshing. Put a paper umbrella in the crushed ice and imagine the tropics.

Crushed ice	1 cup	250 mL
Lime juice	2 tbsp.	30 mL
White rum	1 1/2 oz.	45 mL
Simple Cocktail Syrup, page 10	2 tsp.	10 mL
Grenadine syrup	1 tsp.	5 mL

Pineapple slice, for garnish
Lime slice, cut into quarters, for garnish

Combine first 5 ingredients in cocktail shaker or jar with tight-fitting lid. Shake well. Makes 3/4 cup (175 mL). Pour into 8 oz. (227 mL) glass.

Garnish with fruit. Serves 1.

1 serving: 159 Calories; trace Total Fat; 6 mg Sodium; trace Protein; 17 g Carbohydrate; trace Dietary Fibre

Pictured on page 17.

Strawberry Slush

*A slushy summer favourite! The sweet juiciness of
ripe strawberries with a tang of lime.*

Lemon lime soft drink	1 1/2 cups	375 mL
Frozen whole strawberries, cut up (about 15)	1 1/2 cups	375 mL
Crushed ice	1 cup	250 mL
Granulated sugar	1/4 cup	60 mL

Fresh whole strawberries, for garnish

Measure first 4 ingredients into blender. Process until smooth. Makes
2 2/3 cups (650 mL).

Garnish individual servings with strawberries. Serves 2.

*1 serving: 242 Calories; 0.2 g Total Fat; 25 mg Sodium; 1 g Protein; 63 g Carbohydrate;
3 g Dietary Fibre*

Pictured on page 17.

Simple Cocktail Syrup

*A versatile syrup used for sweet cocktails such as Mai Tai, page 8,
Planter's Punch, page 9, or Singapore Sling, page 11.*

Water	1/2 cup	125 mL
Granulated sugar	1 cup	250 mL

Heat and stir water and sugar in small saucepan on medium-high until
sugar is dissolved. Bring to a boil. Reduce heat to medium-low. Simmer,
uncovered, for 5 minutes. Cool. Store in jar with tight-fitting lid in
refrigerator for up to 6 months. Makes 1 cup (250 mL).

*2 tsp. (10 mL): 33 Calories; 0 g Total Fat; trace Sodium; 0 g Protein; 8 g Carbohydrate;
0 g Dietary Fibre*

Singapore Sling

I've been told that the first sling was created for Somerset Maugham in Raffles in Singapore. This refreshing variation has a lime undertone and a sweet cherry aftertaste.

Crushed ice, to fill glass half full		
Lime juice	2 tsp.	10 mL
Simple Cocktail Syrup, page 10	1 tbsp.	15 mL
Grenadine syrup	1 tbsp.	15 mL
Gin	1 1/2 oz.	45 mL
Cherry whiskey	1/2 oz.	15 mL
Ginger ale	3/4 cup	175 mL

Put crushed ice into 16 oz. (500 mL) glass. Pour lime juice, Simple Cocktail Syrup, grenadine, gin and whiskey over ice.

Add ginger ale. Stir. Serve with swizzle stick and straw. Makes 9 oz. (255 mL). Serves 1.

1 serving: 310 Calories; trace Total Fat; 29 mg Sodium; trace Protein; 47 g Carbohydrate; trace Dietary Fibre

VIRGIN SLING: Omit gin and cherry whiskey.

 To be able to make the most common cocktails, this is a basic list for stocking your cabinet. Start with some basics and add as you experiment with different drinks.

Bourbon	*Tequila*
Brandy	*Vodka*
Gin	*Whiskey*
Peach Schnapps	*Liqueurs (such as Amaretto,*
Rum	*Crème de Cacao, Kahlúa, Baileys*
Scotch	*Irish Cream and Grand Marnier)*

Indian Chai

The fragrant harmony of eastern spices makes this
hot beverage captivating. The warm scents of cardamom,
ginger and cinnamon will delight your nose and your taste buds.

Orange pekoe tea bag	1	1
Milk	2 cups	500 mL
Water	1/2 cup	125 mL
Granulated sugar	4 tsp.	20 mL
Whole green cardamom, bruised (see Note)	6	6
Chopped gingerroot (or 3/4 tsp., 4 mL, ground ginger)	1 tbsp.	15 mL
Cinnamon stick (4 inch, 10 cm, length), crushed	1	1
Dried mint leaves	1/4 tsp.	1 mL
Tea Masala	1/4 – 1/2 tsp.	1 – 2 mL

Combine all 9 ingredients in medium saucepan. Heat on medium for about 10 minutes, stirring occasionally, until beginning to boil. Remove from heat. Strain through fine sieve into 2 mugs. Discard solids. Makes 2 cups (500 mL). Serves 2.

1 serving: 155 Calories; 3 g Total Fat; 138 mg Sodium; 9 g Protein; 24 g Carbohydrate; trace Dietary Fibre

Pictured on page 18.

Note: To bruise cardamom, hit cardamom pods with a mallet or the flat side of a wide knife to "bruise" or crack them open slightly.

 To keep winter drinks warm at a party, serve in a slow cooker on Low setting.

Hazelnut Hot Chocolate

The decadent richness of chocolate with an elegant hint of hazelnut.
This frothy beverage is a dessert in itself.

Milk	2 cups	500 mL
Milk chocolate candy bar, chopped	3 1/2 oz.	100 g
Hazelnut-flavoured liqueur (such as Frangelico)	1/4 cup	60 mL
Whipped cream	1/3 cup	75 mL
Chopped hazelnuts (filberts), toasted (see Tip, page 79)	1 1/2 tbsp.	25 mL
Chocolate sauce	1 tsp.	5 mL

Heat milk in medium saucepan on medium-high for about 3 minutes until small bubbles form around edge and milk is hot. Do not boil. Remove from heat.

Add chocolate and liqueur. Stir until chocolate is melted. Makes 2 1/2 cups (625 mL). Pour into 2 mugs.

Dollop whipped cream onto milk mixture.

Sprinkle with hazelnuts. Drizzle chocolate sauce over top. Serves 2.

1 serving: 584 Calories; 28.4 g Total Fat; 184 mg Sodium; 13 g Protein; 57 g Carbohydrate; 2 g Dietary Fibre

Pictured on page 18.

Paré Pointer
They wanted to go waterskiing but
they couldn't find a lake with a slope.

Bistro Milk

A steamed milk beverage similar to what you find in trendy coffee shops—no steam machine required! Perfect for soothing the nerves before bed.

Skim milk	1 1/3 cups	325 mL
White corn syrup	3 tbsp.	50 mL
Clear vanilla	1 1/2 – 2 tsp.	7 – 10 mL
Ground cinnamon, sprinkle (optional)		

Heat milk and corn syrup in small saucepan until hot. Do not boil. Remove from heat.

Add vanilla. Whisk until frothy or use milk frother. Pour into mug.

Sprinkle with cinnamon. Serves 1.

1 serving: 331 Calories; 0.6 g Total Fat; 221 mg Sodium; 12 g Protein; 68 g Carbohydrate; 0 g Dietary Fibre

ALMOND BISTRO MILK: Omit vanilla. Add 1/8 to 1/4 tsp. (0.5 to 1 mL) almond flavouring.

Maple Milk

Warm your soul with this hot, comforting beverage.
A subtle maple flavour with a hint of cloves to ebb your cares away.

Milk	2 cups	500 mL
Maple syrup	1/4 cup	60 mL
Cinnamon stick (4 inch, 10 cm, length)	1	1
Whole cloves	4	4
Granulated sugar	2 tsp.	10 mL

Combine all 5 ingredients in medium saucepan. Heat and stir on medium for 5 minutes. Remove from heat. Let stand for 10 minutes. Strain. Discard solids. Return to same pan. Heat and stir milk mixture for 2 to 3 minutes until hot. Makes about 2 1/4 cups (550 mL). Pour into 2 mugs. Serves 2.

1 serving: 234 Calories; 2.8 g Total Fat; 133 mg Sodium; 8 g Protein; 45 g Carbohydrate; 0 g Dietary Fibre

Sweet Pineapple Tea

*The complementary flavours of pineapple and honey will tingle your
taste buds and awaken your senses. Serve hot to soothe a sore throat.
Also delicious over ice and topped with a maraschino cherry.*

Boiling water	2 cups	500 mL
Orange pekoe tea bag	1	1
Pineapple juice, warmed	1/2 cup	125 mL
Liquid honey	1 – 2 tbsp.	15 – 30 mL
Lemon juice (optional)	1/2 tsp.	2 mL
Cinnamon sticks (4 inch, 10 cm, lengths)	2	2

Pour boiling water over tea bag in small teapot. Let steep for 10 minutes.
Squeeze and discard tea bag.

Add pineapple juice, honey and lemon juice. Stir. Pour into 2 mugs.

Add 1 cinnamon stick to each for stirring. Makes 2 1/2 cups (625 mL).
Serves 2.

*1 serving: 72 Calories; 0.1 g Total Fat; 9 mg Sodium; trace Protein; 19 g Carbohydrate;
trace Dietary Fibre*

Pictured on page 18.

COLD PINEAPPLE TEA: Prepare as above but in 4 cup (1 L) glass liquid
measure. Add cinnamon sticks. Chill. Remove cinnamon sticks. Pour over
ice cubes in glasses. Add 1 cinnamon stick to each, if desired.

Paré Pointer

*They hoped their plane didn't travel faster than sound.
They wanted to have a visit while flying.*

Bartender's Iced Tea

A tall and delicious "tea-less" iced tea. This citrusy beverage is refreshing and summery. Enjoy beside the pool or on your shaded deck.

Ice cubes	3	3
Vodka	1 tbsp.	15 mL
Gin	1 tbsp.	15 mL
White rum	1 tbsp.	15 mL
Orange-flavoured liqueur (such as Grand Marnier)	1 tbsp.	15 mL
Lemonade	1 cup	250 mL
Cola beverage	2 tbsp.	30 mL

Put ice cubes into tall 16 oz. (500 mL) glass. Pour vodka, gin, rum and liqueur over ice cubes.

Add lemonade and cola. Stir. Makes 1 1/2 cups (375 mL). Serves 1.

1 serving: 279 Calories; 0.1 g Total Fat; 11 mg Sodium; trace Protein; 38 g Carbohydrate; 0 g Dietary Fibre

1. Planter's Punch, page 9
2. Fluffy Duck, page 8
3. Strawberry Slush, page 10
4. Mai Tai, page 8

Cherry Tea Float

A summer drink that is full of cherry fun! This frothy, fruity beverage is both rich and refreshing. It's like a dressed-up float!

Boiling water	3/4 cup	175 mL
Orange pekoe tea bag	1	1
Chilled maraschino cherry syrup	1/4 cup	60 mL
Chilled lemon lime soft drink	1/2 cup	125 mL
Maraschino cherries	2	2
Scoop of vanilla ice cream (about 1/2 cup, 125 mL)	1	1

Pour boiling water over tea bag in small teapot. Let steep for 10 minutes. Squeeze and discard tea bag. Pour tea into 2 cup (500 mL) liquid measure. Chill.

Add cherry syrup and soft drink. Stir well.

Put cherries into tall 16 oz. (500 mL) glass. Add ice cream. Slowly pour tea mixture over ice cream. Foam will form. Serve with long spoon and straw. Makes about 1 1/2 cups (375 mL). Serves 1.

1 serving: 274 Calories; 7.8 g Total Fat; 76 mg Sodium; 3 g Protein; 51 g Carbohydrate; 1 g Dietary Fibre

1. Hazelnut Hot Chocolate, page 13
2. Indian Chai, page 12
3. Sweet Pineapple Tea, page 15

Props Courtesy Of: Anchor Hocking Canada

Oatmeal Cake

A mildly spiced oatmeal cake with a chewy, nutty topping. A perfect snacking cake.

Rolled oats (not instant)	1 cup	250 mL
Boiling water	1 cup	250 mL
Large eggs	2	2
Granulated sugar	1 cup	250 mL
Cooking oil	1/2 cup	125 mL
Vanilla	1 tsp.	5 mL
All-purpose flour	1 1/3 cups	325 mL
Baking soda	1 1/2 tsp.	7 mL
Ground cinnamon	1 tsp.	5 mL
Salt	1/2 tsp.	2 mL
TOPPING		
Hard margarine (or butter)	1/4 cup	60 mL
Brown sugar, packed	2/3 cup	150 mL
Half-and-half cream (or milk)	2 tbsp.	30 mL
Chopped pecans (or walnuts)	1/2 cup	125 mL
Medium coconut	1/2 cup	125 mL

Measure rolled oats into small bowl. Pour boiling water over top. Stir. Let stand, uncovered, for 20 minutes.

Beat eggs in large bowl until frothy. Add sugar. Beat. Add cooking oil and vanilla. Beat until well combined.

Combine flour, baking soda, cinnamon and salt in separate small bowl. Add flour mixture to egg mixture in 3 additions, alternating with oatmeal mixture in 2 additions, beginning and ending with flour mixture. Turn into greased 9 x 9 inch (22 x 22 cm) pan. Spread evenly. Bake in 350°F (175°C) oven for about 30 minutes until wooden pick inserted in centre comes out clean.

Topping: Mix all 5 ingredients in small saucepan. Heat and stir on medium-low until margarine is melted and brown sugar is dissolved. Do not boil. Spread over cake. Bake for 5 to 7 minutes until top bubbles all over. Cuts into 16 pieces.

1 piece: 302 Calories; 16.2 g Total Fat; 244 mg Sodium; 3 g Protein; 37 g Carbohydrate; 1 g Dietary Fibre

Pictured on page 35.

Pineapple Mini-Cakes

Cinnamon-flecked pineapple dresses up a simple white cake recipe.
A perfect, light dessert.

Can of crushed pineapple, drained	14 oz.	398 mL
Hard margarine (or butter), softened	1/4 cup	60 mL
Brown sugar, packed	1/2 cup	125 mL
Ground cinnamon	1 tsp.	5 mL
Large egg	1	1
Granulated sugar	2 tbsp.	30 mL
Hard margarine (or butter), softened	1/4 cup	60 mL
Milk	1 cup	250 mL
All-purpose flour	2 cups	500 mL
Baking powder	1 tbsp.	15 mL
Salt	1/2 tsp.	2 mL

Combine first 4 ingredients in medium bowl. Divide evenly and spoon into 12 greased muffin cups.

Beat egg, granulated sugar and second amount of margarine in small bowl. Add milk. Mix.

Combine flour, baking powder and salt in large bowl. Make a well in centre. Pour milk mixture into well. Stir until just moistened. Divide evenly and spoon onto pineapple mixture. Bake in 400°F (205°C) oven for about 18 minutes until wooden pick inserted in centre comes out clean. Invert immediately onto wire rack to cool. There will be some stickiness on bottom. Makes 12 mini-cakes.

1 mini-cake: 224 Calories; 9 g Total Fat; 307 mg Sodium; 4 g Protein; 33 g Carbohydrate; 1 g Dietary Fibre

Chocolate Snack Cake

*A rich chocolate cake from mixing bowl to dessert plate in less than 30 minutes!
The most difficult part is limiting yourself to one piece! Delicious with
a scoop of ice cream and a drizzle of caramel or hot fudge sauce.*

Hard margarine (or butter), softened	2 tbsp.	30 mL
Granulated sugar	1/2 cup	125 mL
Large egg	1	1
Milk	1/3 cup	75 mL
Vanilla	1/2 tsp.	2 mL
All-purpose flour	2/3 cup	150 mL
Cocoa, sifted if lumpy	2 tbsp.	30 mL
Baking powder	1/2 tsp.	2 mL
Baking soda	1/2 tsp.	2 mL
Salt	1/4 tsp.	1 mL

Beat first 5 ingredients together in medium bowl.

Add flour, cocoa, baking powder, baking soda and salt. Beat until smooth.
Turn into greased 9 × 9 inch (22 × 22 cm) pan. Bake in 350°F (175°C) oven
for about 14 minutes until wooden pick inserted in centre comes out clean.
Cool. Cuts into 9 pieces as a dessert or 12 pieces as a snack.

*1 piece: 120 Calories; 3.5 g Total Fat; 200 mg Sodium; 2 g Protein; 20 g Carbohydrate;
1 g Dietary Fibre*

Cola Zucchini Cake

*This unlikely combination of ingredients makes a surprisingly rich
and chocolatey cake. It is deliciously moist and speckled with
chocolate chips throughout. Drizzle with White Chocolate
Sauce, page 111, for a special occasion.*

Devil's food cake mix (2 layer size)	1	1
Cola beverage	1/2 cup	125 mL
Large eggs	3	3
Cooking oil	1/3 cup	75 mL

(continued on next page)

Cakes

| Grated zucchini, with peel | 1 1/2 cups | 375 mL |
| Semi-sweet chocolate chips | 1 cup | 250 mL |

Empty cake mix into large bowl. Add cola, eggs and cooking oil. Beat on low until just moistened. Beat on medium for 2 minutes.

Add zucchini. Stir. Turn into greased 9 x 13 inch (22 x 33 cm) pan.

Sprinkle with chocolate chips. Bake in 350°F (175°C) oven for 35 to 40 minutes until wooden pick inserted in centre comes out clean. Cool. Cuts into 24 pieces.

1 piece: 170 Calories; 9.5 g Total Fat; 189 mg Sodium; 2 g Protein; 21 g Carbohydrate; 1 g Dietary Fibre

Pictured on page 107.

White Snack Cake

This versatile snacking cake is so easy to prepare and can be enjoyed in so many ways. Serve with a scoop of ice cream, a spoonful of your favourite pie filling or with hot caramel or fudge sauce. Use your imagination to create other dessert sensations.

Hard margarine (or butter), softened	1 tbsp.	15 mL
Granulated sugar	1/3 cup	75 mL
Large egg	1	1
Vanilla	1/2 tsp.	2 mL
Milk	1/4 cup	60 mL
All-purpose flour	1/2 cup	125 mL
Baking powder	1/2 tsp.	2 mL
Salt	1/8 tsp.	0.5 mL

Beat first 5 ingredients together in medium bowl.

Add flour, baking powder and salt. Beat until smooth. Turn into greased 8 x 8 inch (20 x 20 cm) pan. Bake in 350°F (175°C) oven for about 12 minutes until wooden pick inserted in centre comes out clean. Cool. Cuts into 9 pieces as a dessert or 12 pieces as a snack.

1 piece: 81 Calories; 2 g Total Fat; 81 mg Sodium; 2 g Protein; 14 g Carbohydrate; trace Dietary Fibre

Lemon Poppy Loaf

This moist, lemony loaf has a melt-in-your-mouth, creamy icing that will have your guests lining up for seconds. Enjoy with a nice cup of tea or coffee.

Granulated sugar	3/4 cup	175 mL
Hard margarine (or butter), softened	6 tbsp.	100 mL
Finely grated lemon zest	1 tbsp.	15 mL
Large eggs	3	3
All-purpose flour	1 1/2 cups	375 mL
Baking powder	2 tsp.	10 mL
Medium coconut	3/4 cup	175 mL
Poppy seeds	6 tbsp.	100 mL
Sour cream	6 tbsp.	100 mL
Milk	6 tbsp.	100 mL
LEMON CREAM CHEESE ICING		
Block of cream cheese, softened	4 oz.	125 g
Finely grated lemon zest	2 tsp.	10 mL
Icing (confectioner's) sugar	1 1/2 cups	375 mL
Long thread coconut, toasted (see Tip, page 79)	1/4 cup	60 mL

Beat first 4 ingredients in medium bowl until light and fluffy. Mixture may look curdled.

Stir flour and baking powder into margarine mixture.

Add next 4 ingredients. Mix well. Spread in greased 8 x 4 x 3 inch (20 x 10 x 7.5 cm) loaf pan. Bake in 350°F (175°C) oven for about 1 hour until wooden pick inserted in centre comes out clean. Let stand in pan for 10 minutes before turning out onto wire rack to cool.

Lemon Cream Cheese Icing: Beat cream cheese, lemon zest and icing sugar in medium bowl until light and fluffy. Makes about 1 cup (250 mL) icing. Spread over top of loaf.

Sprinkle with coconut. Cuts into 16 slices.

1 slice: 278 Calories; 14.3 g Total Fat; 141 mg Sodium; 4 g Protein; 35 g Carbohydrate; 1 g Dietary Fibre

Pictured on page 108 and on back cover.

Cakes

Cherry Snack Cake

This fun, rosy-coloured cake makes a fabulous child's birthday cake—especially with the cherries and chocolate chips throughout. Who found the only whole cherry?

Hard margarine (or butter), softened	1/2 cup	125 mL
Granulated sugar	1 cup	250 mL
Large eggs	2	2
Vanilla	1 tsp.	5 mL
Semi-sweet chocolate baking square, grated	1 oz.	28 g
Chopped maraschino cherries	1/4 cup	60 mL
Whole maraschino cherry	1	1
All-purpose flour	1 1/2 cups	375 mL
Baking powder	1 1/2 tsp.	7 mL
Salt	1/4 tsp.	1 mL
Maraschino cherry syrup	1/4 cup	60 mL
Icing (confectioner's) sugar, for dusting		

Cream margarine and granulated sugar in large bowl. Beat in eggs, 1 at a time, beating well after each addition.

Add vanilla, chocolate and cherries. Stir.

Mix flour, baking powder and salt in small bowl.

Add flour mixture to margarine mixture in 3 additions, alternating with cherry syrup in 2 additions, beginning and ending with flour mixture. Spread in greased 9 × 9 inch (22 × 22 cm) pan. Bake in 350°F (175°C) oven for about 35 minutes until wooden pick inserted in centre comes out clean. Cool.

Dust individual servings with icing sugar. Cuts into 9 pieces as a dessert or 12 pieces as a snack.

1 piece: 318 Calories; 13 g Total Fat; 269 mg Sodium; 4 g Protein; 47 g Carbohydrate; 1 g Dietary Fibre

Pictured on page 36.

Raisin Cake

Enjoy bursts of natural sweetness from the raisins in this simple spice cake.
And who can resist the velvety smooth cream cheese icing?

All-purpose flour	2 1/2 cups	625 mL
Brown sugar, packed	2/3 cup	150 mL
Baking powder	1 tbsp.	15 mL
Baking soda	1 tsp.	5 mL
Ground cinnamon	1 tsp.	5 mL
Ground ginger	1/2 tsp.	2 mL
Ground nutmeg	1/4 tsp.	1 mL
Hard margarine (or butter), softened	1/2 cup	125 mL
Large eggs	2	2
Can of raisin pie filling	19 oz.	540 mL
Vanilla	1 1/2 tsp.	7 mL
CREAM CHEESE ICING		
Spreadable cream cheese	1/4 cup	60 mL
Hard margarine (or butter), softened	1 tbsp.	15 mL
Vanilla	1/2 tsp.	2 mL
Icing (confectioner's) sugar	2 cups	500 mL
Milk	8 tsp.	40 mL

Measure first 7 ingredients into large bowl. Stir. Make a well in centre.

Add margarine, eggs, pie filling and vanilla to well. Beat on low until just moistened. Beat on medium for 3 minutes. Spread in greased 9 × 13 inch (22 × 33 cm) pan. Bake in 350°F (175°C) oven for 35 to 40 minutes until wooden pick inserted in centre comes out clean. Cool in pan on wire rack.

Cream Cheese Icing: Beat cream cheese, margarine and vanilla until light and fluffy.

Add icing sugar, 1/2 cup (125 mL) at a time, beating well after each addition. Beat in milk, 1 tsp. (5 mL) at a time, until spreadable consistency. Spread over top of cooled cake. Cuts into 24 pieces.

1 piece: 202 Calories; 6.1 g Total Fat; 172 mg Sodium; 2 g Protein; 35 g Carbohydrate; 1 g Dietary Fibre

Pictured on page 35.

Almond Peach Little Cakes

These buttery, little, almond-flavoured cakes are delicious with the sweet, summery taste of peaches. Or try with fresh blueberries or raspberries in season. Individually freeze and thaw as needed.

Almond meal (ground almonds)	1 cup	250 mL
Hard margarine (or butter), melted	3/4 cup	175 mL
Egg whites (large), fork-beaten	6	6
Icing (confectioner's) sugar	1 1/2 cups	375 mL
All-purpose flour	1/2 cup	125 mL
Finely chopped peaches (about 1/2 of 14 oz., 398 mL, can, drained)	1/2 cup	125 mL

Icing (confectioner's) sugar, for dusting

Stir first 5 ingredients in large bowl until just combined. Divide evenly and spoon into 12 well-greased muffin cups 1/2 full.

Divide and scatter peaches onto batter. Bake in 375°F (190°C) oven for about 25 minutes until wooden pick inserted in centre comes out clean. Let stand in pan for 10 minutes before turning out onto wire rack to cool.

Dust with icing sugar. Makes 12 little cakes.

1 little cake: 236 Calories; 15.1 g Total Fat; 170 mg Sodium; 4 g Protein; 23 g Carbohydrate; trace Dietary Fibre

Pictured on page 35.

Paré Pointer

The real reason climbers are tied together with rope is so no one can decide to go home.

Cherry Mini-Cakes

Moist, cherry-flavoured tea cakes with crunchy pecans and chewy cherries.

Hard margarine (or butter), softened	1/2 cup	125 mL
Brown sugar, packed	1 cup	250 mL
Granulated sugar	1/4 cup	60 mL
Large eggs, fork-beaten	2	2
Almond flavouring	1/2 tsp.	2 mL
Apple juice	1/4 cup	60 mL
All-purpose flour	1 2/3 cups	400 mL
Baking powder	1 tsp.	5 mL
Salt	1/2 tsp.	2 mL
Chopped pecans (or walnuts)	1/3 cup	75 mL
Chopped glazed cherries	1/2 cup	125 mL

Icing (confectioner's) sugar, for dusting

Beat first 6 ingredients together in large bowl until well combined.

Combine flour, baking powder and salt in medium bowl. Add to margarine mixture. Mix until no dry flour remains.

Sprinkle 1 tsp. (5 mL) pecans and 2 tsp. (10 mL) cherries each into bottom of 12 greased muffin cups. Divide evenly and spoon batter over top. Bake in 400°F (205°C) oven for 18 to 20 minutes until wooden pick inserted in centre comes out clean. Let stand in pan for 5 minutes before turning out onto wire rack to cool.

Dust with icing sugar. Makes 12 mini-cakes.

1 mini-cake: 293 Calories; 11.4 g Total Fat; 243 mg Sodium; 3 g Protein; 46 g Carbohydrate; 1 g Dietary Fibre

Candies & Confections

Candy-Making Tips:

- Use a candy thermometer to take the guesswork out of candy making. Test your candy thermometer before each use. Bring cold water to a boil. Candy thermometer should read 212°F (100°C) in boiling water at sea level. Adjust recipe temperature up or down based on test results. For example, if your thermometer reads 206°F (97°C), subtract 6°F (3°C) from each temperature called for in recipe. Double check with the cold water test.

- Do not alter any ingredient amounts or double or halve candy recipes.

- Use a good quality mixing spoon and be prepared to use your muscles for stirring.

Candy Thermometer Chart

Stage	Temperature	Until small amount dropped into cold water...
Thread	223° to 234°F 106° to 112°C	forms a soft 2 inch (5 cm) thread.
Soft ball	234° to 240°F 112° to 116°C	forms a soft ball that flattens on its own accord when removed.
Firm ball	242° to 248°F 117° to 120°C	forms a pliable ball.
Hard ball	250° to 265°F 120° to 129°C	forms a rigid ball that is still somewhat pliable.
Soft crack	270° to 290°F 132° to 143°C	separates into hard, but pliable, threads.
Hard crack	300° to 310°F 150° to 154°C	separates into hard, brittle threads.

Raspberry Turkish Jellies

A fruity variation on the ever-popular Turkish Delight.
These deep red jellies are ideal for satisfying after-dinner sweet cravings.
As beautiful as they are delicious.

Water	1 cup	250 mL
Granulated sugar	1 3/4 cups	425 mL
Sweetened powdered raspberry-flavoured drink crystals (see Note)	1/4 cup	60 mL
Lemon juice	1 tbsp.	15 mL
Cold water	3/4 cup	175 mL
Envelopes of unflavoured gelatin (1/4 oz., 7 g, each)	5	5
Fine granulated sugar	3 tbsp.	50 mL

Stir water, first amount of sugar, drink crystals and lemon juice in large saucepan. Bring to a boil on medium. Boil for 3 to 4 minutes, stirring occasionally, until sugar is dissolved.

Stir cold water and gelatin in small bowl. Let stand for 1 minute. Add to boiling syrup mixture. Heat and stir for about 1 minute until gelatin is dissolved. Reduce heat to medium-low or just enough to keep syrup at a steady boil. Boil slowly, uncovered, without stirring, for about 40 minutes until mixture reaches soft ball stage (about 235°F, 113°C, on candy thermometer) or until small amount dropped into very cold water forms a soft ball that flattens on its own accord when removed. Dampen 8 x 8 inch (20 x 20 cm) or 9 x 9 inch (22 x 22 cm) pan with cold water. Immediately pour syrup mixture into pan. Let stand, uncovered, at room temperature for at least 24 hours until very firm.

Put second amount of sugar in separate small bowl. To remove jellies from pan, coat long sharp knife with sugar and cut along sides of pan. Cut into 4 more-manageable portions, coating edge of knife before each cut. Pull jelly sections from pan, 1 at a time, and place on work surface coated with sugar. Sprinkle sugar as needed to prevent sticking. Cut jellies into 1 inch (2.5 cm) pieces with edge of knife coated in sugar and press straight down to cut through. Coat individual jellies on all sides with sugar. Store for up to 4 weeks with sugar in between layers in airtight container. Makes about 1 1/4 lbs. (560 g). Cuts into about 80 jellies.

(continued on next page)

Candies & Confections

1 jelly: 25 Calories; 0 g Total Fat; 1 mg Sodium; trace Protein; 6 g Carbohydrate; 0 g Dietary Fibre

Pictured on front cover.

Note: Any flavour of sweetened powdered drink crystals, such as passion fruit, kiwifruit, cranberry, grape, orange or lemonade, can be used.

Variation: Omit second amount of sugar. Use icing sugar to coat individual jellies.

Candied Peanuts And Dates

These candied peanuts and dates have something to satisfy a variety of cravings—they are sweet, chewy, crunchy and chocolatey.

Butter (not margarine)	6 tbsp.	100 mL
Brown sugar, packed	3 tbsp.	50 mL
Corn syrup	2 tbsp.	30 mL
Unsalted peanuts	1 cup	250 mL
Finely chopped dates	1/2 cup	125 mL
Box of candy-coated chocolate candies (such as Smarties)	2 oz.	56 g

Heat butter, brown sugar and corn syrup in large saucepan on medium until bubbly.

Add peanuts and dates. Heat and stir for about 3 minutes until peanuts are coated and mixture is slightly thickened. Remove from heat. Let stand for 15 to 20 minutes to cool. If mixture cools too much, it will be difficult to mix in candies.

Stir in candies. Press in greased foil-lined 8 × 8 inch (20 × 20 cm) pan. Cool completely. Cuts into 24 triangles.

1 triangle: 97 Calories; 6.7 g Total Fat; 34 mg Sodium; 2 g Protein; 9 g Carbohydrate; 1 g Dietary Fibre

Pictured on page 126.

Candy Fruit Balls

These chewy fruit and nut balls are so delicious you won't notice how healthy they are! Excellent packed into the kids' lunches or as a snack while hiking.

Hard margarine (or butter)	2/3 cup	150 mL
Granulated sugar	1 cup	250 mL
Chopped dried apricots	1/2 cup	125 mL
Chopped dates	1/2 cup	125 mL
Vanilla	1/2 tsp.	2 mL
Crisp rice cereal	2 cups	500 mL
Chopped walnuts (or pecans)	1/2 cup	125 mL
Granulated (or icing, confectioner's) sugar	1/4 cup	60 mL

Combine first 4 ingredients in large saucepan. Heat and stir on medium for 5 minutes until fruit is soft. Remove from heat.

Add vanilla, cereal and walnuts. Stir well. Cool until able to handle. Shape into 1 inch (2.5 cm) balls.

Put second amount of sugar into resealable plastic bag. Drop, a few balls at a time, into sugar. Shake until well coated. Makes about 40 fruit balls.

1 fruit ball: 79 Calories; 4.2 g Total Fat; 53 mg Sodium; 1 g Protein; 10 g Carbohydrate; trace Dietary Fibre

Pictured on page 143.

 Most candies will store for 2 to 3 weeks in an airtight container in a cool, dry place. Be sure to store only one kind of candy in each container or the texture and flavour might change. Protect individual candies by covering with plastic wrap or store in between layers of waxed paper. If you want to freeze candies, store in a resealable freezer bag or airtight container.

Candies & Confections

Spiced Candied Almonds

The delicious taste of toasted almonds, candied and spiced with nutmeg and allspice. It's hard to stop once you start!

GLAZE		
Granulated sugar	1 1/2 cups	375 mL
Water	1/4 cup	60 mL
Ground nutmeg	1/2 tsp.	2 mL
Ground allspice	1/4 tsp.	1 mL
Salt	3/4 tsp.	4 mL
Whole almonds (see Note), toasted (see Tip, page 79)	1 cup	250 mL

Glaze: Heat and stir sugar and water in large heavy saucepan or frying pan on medium. Brush side of saucepan with damp pastry brush to prevent any sugar crystals from forming. Boil slowly, uncovered, without stirring, until sugar is melted and mixture is light caramel colour. Remove from heat.

Stir in nutmeg, allspice and salt. Mixture will foam a bit. Drizzle over almonds on lightly greased 11 × 17 inch (28 × 43 cm) baking sheet being sure to get some on each one. Candy will not fill pan. Cool completely. Break into bite-size pieces. Makes about 14 oz. (395 g).

1 oz. (28 g): 151 Calories; 5.6 g Total Fat; 129 mg Sodium; 2 g Protein; 25 g Carbohydrate; 1 g Dietary Fibre

Note: Almonds with or without the skins work fine. You may even want to use a mix of both.

Paré Pointer

Her eyes have never been checked. They have always been brown.

Macadamia Nut Toffee

A crunchy, nutty, oven-baked toffee that doesn't require a candy thermometer. For a more economical, but equally delicious, variation, try with peanuts.

Butter (not margarine)	2/3 cup	150 mL
Brown sugar, packed	1 cup	250 mL
Coarsely chopped macadamia nuts	1 cup	250 mL
Semi-sweet chocolate chips	1/2 cup	125 mL
Finely chopped macadamia nuts	1/4 cup	60 mL

Stir butter and brown sugar in small saucepan on medium until boiling and sugar is dissolved.

Stir in first amount of nuts. Pour into greased 9 x 9 inch (22 x 22 cm) pan. Bake in 375°F (190°C) oven for about 15 minutes until caramel coloured and entire surface is covered with small bubbles. Let stand in pan on wire rack for 5 minutes to cool slightly.

Sprinkle with chocolate chips. Let stand for about 5 minutes until chocolate chips are melted. Spread evenly.

Sprinkle with second amount of nuts while chocolate is still warm. Cool completely. Makes 1 lb., 2 oz. (511 g). Breaks into about 64 pieces.

1 piece: 55 Calories; 4.1 g Total Fat; 23 mg Sodium; trace Protein; 5 g Carbohydrate; trace Dietary Fibre

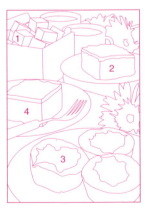

1. Butter Pecan Pudding Fudge, page 41
2. Raisin Cake, page 26
3. Almond Peach Little Cakes, page 27
4. Oatmeal Cake, page 20

Props courtesy of: Wiltshire ®

Candies & Confections

Seed And Honey Fruit Plums

This no-bake sweet treat is so easy and so healthy. A perfect blend of dried fruit, honey and coconut. A popular after-school snack for kids.

Small navel orange, with peel	1	1
Dried figs, stems removed, packed	1/4 cup	60 mL
Whole dates, packed	1/4 cup	60 mL
Dried apricots, packed	1/4 cup	60 mL
Seedless raisins	1/4 cup	60 mL
Liquid honey	2 tbsp.	30 mL
Roasted sunflower seeds	1/4 cup	60 mL
Long thread coconut, toasted (see Tip, page 79)	1/2 cup	125 mL

Cut off and discard 1/2 inch (12 mm) from top and bottom of orange. Cut remainder of orange into quarters.

Put orange into food processor fitted with chopping blade. Add next 6 ingredients. Pulse with on/off motion in 3 to 4 second bursts until coarsely chopped. Process for 30 seconds until finely chopped. Food grinder may also be used. Shape into balls, using 2 tsp. (10 mL) for each ball.

Place coconut in shallow dish or on waxed paper. Roll balls to coat well. Makes about 28 balls.

1 ball: 41 Calories; 1.8 g Total Fat; 1 mg Sodium; 1 g Protein; 7 g Carbohydrate; 1 g Dietary Fibre

Pictured on page 53.

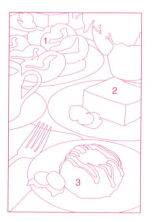

1. Spiced Palmiers, page 87
2. Cherry Snack Cake, page 25
3. A Touch Of Danish, page 94

Props Courtesy Of: Pfaltzgraff Canada

Chocolate Fudge

Who can resist a rich, creamy, dark, melt-in-your-mouth fudge?
Your guests will ask for a small piece, but they'll be back for another.

Brown sugar, packed	1 1/2 cups	375 mL
Granulated sugar	1 1/2 cups	375 mL
Milk	1 cup	250 mL
Corn syrup	3 tbsp.	50 mL
Unsweetened chocolate baking squares (1 oz., 28 g, each), cut up	3	3
Salt	1/8 tsp.	0.5 mL
Hard margarine (or butter)	2 tbsp.	30 mL
Vanilla	1 tsp.	5 mL

Combine first 6 ingredients in large heavy saucepan. Heat and stir on medium until chocolate is melted and mixture begins to boil. Reduce heat to medium-low. Brush side of saucepan with damp pastry brush to allow any sugar crystals on side of saucepan to dissolve. Boil slowly, uncovered, without stirring, until mixture reaches soft ball stage (about 238°F, 114°C, on candy thermometer) or until small amount dropped into very cold water forms a soft ball that flattens on its own accord when removed. Remove from heat. Chocolate will mix in when beaten later.

Add margarine and vanilla. Stir. Let stand for 20 minutes. Beat for about 2 minutes until just beginning to thicken, glossy look disappears and looks creamy. Turn quickly into greased 8 x 8 inch (20 x 20 cm) pan. Spread evenly. Cut while barely warm. Keep well covered to prevent drying. Makes about 1 1/2 lbs. (680 g). Cuts into 64 pieces.

1 piece: 55 Calories; 1.1 g Total Fat; 14 mg Sodium; trace Protein; 12 g Carbohydrate; trace Dietary Fibre

CHOCOLATE NUT FUDGE: Stir in 1/2 cup (125 mL) finely chopped walnuts (or pecans) just prior to turning into pan.

Peanut Butter Fudge

A peanut butter lover's delight. This creamy and peanutty fudge looks and smells as delicious as it tastes.

Granulated sugar	2 cups	500 mL
Hard margarine (or butter)	3 tbsp.	50 mL
Milk	1/2 cup	125 mL
Salt, just a pinch		
Smooth peanut butter	1/2 cup	125 mL
Marshmallow creme	1/2 cup	125 mL
Vanilla	1/2 tsp.	2 mL

Combine sugar, margarine, milk and salt in large heavy saucepan. Heat and stir on medium until sugar is dissolved and mixture begins to boil. Reduce heat to medium-low. Boil slowly, uncovered, for about 8 minutes, stirring twice, until mixture reaches soft ball stage (about 235°F, 113°C, on candy thermometer) or until small amount dropped into very cold water forms a soft ball that flattens on its own accord when removed. Remove from heat. Let stand for 10 minutes.

Stir in peanut butter, marshmallow creme and vanilla. Pour into greased 8 × 8 inch (20 × 20 cm) pan. Spread evenly. Cool. Makes about 1 1/2 lbs. (680 g). Cuts into 64 pieces.

1 piece: 50 Calories; 1.7 g Total Fat; 18 mg Sodium; 1 g Protein; 9 g Carbohydrate; trace Dietary Fibre

Paré Pointer

Tennis is such a noisy game. You have to raise a "racket" to play.

Burnt Sugar Fudge

Smooth and creamy with a subtle burnt sugar caramel flavour.
Keep this recipe handy—there will be requests for repeats!

Granulated sugar	1 cup	250 mL
Water	1/4 cup	60 mL
Half-and-half cream (or evaporated milk)	1 cup	250 mL
Granulated sugar	2 cups	500 mL
Hard margarine (or butter)	3 tbsp.	50 mL
Vanilla	1 tsp.	5 mL
Chopped pecans (or walnuts)	3/4 cup	175 mL

Grease side of large heavy saucepan. Place first amount of sugar in saucepan. Heat and stir on medium until sugar is melted and rich brown in colour. Remove from heat.

Gradually, and very carefully, stir in water. Mixture will sputter furiously and sugar may start to solidify. Return to heat. Add cream, second amount of sugar and margarine. Heat and stir on medium until boiling and caramelized sugar is dissolved. Reduce heat to medium-low. Brush side of saucepan with damp pastry brush to allow any sugar crystals on side of saucepan to dissolve. Boil slowly, uncovered, for about 30 minutes, stirring frequently, until mixture reaches soft ball stage (about 240°F, 116°C, on candy thermometer) or until small amount dropped into very cold water forms a soft ball that flattens on its own accord when removed. Remove from heat. Let stand for 20 minutes.

Stir in vanilla and pecans. Beat on low until very thick and difficult to beat further. Turn into greased 9 x 9 inch (22 x 22 cm) pan. Spread evenly. Cool. Makes about 1 3/4 lbs. (790 g). Cuts into 64 pieces.

1 piece: 58 Calories; 1.9 g Total Fat; 8 mg Sodium; trace Protein; 10 g Carbohydrate; trace Dietary Fibre

Candies & Confections

Butter Pecan Pudding Fudge

The classic flavour of butter pecan makes this rich, creamy fudge extraordinary!
This simple microwave fudge recipe requires no candy thermometer and is
prepared in just a few minutes. Store this soft fudge in the refrigerator.

Chopped pecans	1/2 cup	125 mL
Butter (not margarine)	2 tsp.	10 mL
Milk	1/3 cup	75 mL
Vanilla	1 tsp.	5 mL
Butterscotch pudding powder (not instant), 6 serving size	1	1
Butter (not margarine)	3 tbsp.	50 mL
Icing (confectioner's) sugar	2 1/2 cups	625 mL

Fry pecans in first amount of butter in small frying pan until browned.
Set aside.

Whisk milk, vanilla and pudding powder in large microwave-safe bowl until
smooth. Add second amount of butter. Microwave, uncovered, on high
(100%) for 1 minute. Whisk until smooth. Microwave on high (100%) for
30 seconds. Whisk. Microwave on high (100%) for 50 to 60 seconds until
just beginning to bubble on side of bowl. Whisk. Do not overcook.

Immediately whisk in icing sugar until thickened. Stir in pecan mixture.
Pack into greased foil-lined 9 x 5 x 3 inch (22 x 12.5 x 7.5 cm) loaf pan.
Cover with plastic wrap. Chill for 1 hour before serving. Makes about
1 lb. (454 g). Cuts into 40 pieces.

1 piece: 67 Calories; 2.2 g Total Fat; 27 mg Sodium; trace Protein; 12 g Carbohydrate;
trace Dietary Fibre

Pictured on page 35.

Instant Maple Walnut Fudge

A rich fudge that is quick and easy to make.

Butterscotch chips	1 1/2 cups	375 mL
Semi-sweet chocolate chips	1/2 cup	125 mL
Container of vanilla frosting	16 oz.	450 g
Maple flavouring	1/4 tsp.	1 mL
Chopped walnuts	1 cup	250 mL

Heat butterscotch and chocolate chips in medium saucepan on lowest heat until almost melted. Do not overheat. Remove from heat. Stir until smooth.

Stir in frosting, flavouring and walnuts. Pour into greased foil-lined 8 x 8 inch (20 x 20 cm) pan. Spread evenly. Chill, uncovered, for about 45 minutes until firm. Remove fudge and foil from pan. Remove and discard foil. Makes about 1 1/2 lbs. (680 g). Cuts into 64 pieces.

1 piece: 63 Calories; 2.9 g Total Fat; 9 mg Sodium; 1 g Protein; 9 g Carbohydrate; trace Dietary Fibre

Pictured on front cover.

 To reduce frustration when making candy, be sure to read the entire recipe before you begin. Collect the ingredients and tools you will need (such as candy thermometer and a cup for cold water) and make sure you have the exact measurements. Keep everything close by and handy.

English Toffee

A smooth, hard toffee with a delicious caramel flavour.
Suck on it slowly and savour its richness.

Brown sugar, packed	1 cup	250 mL
Granulated sugar	1 cup	250 mL
Half-and-half cream	1/2 cup	125 mL
Butter (not margarine)	1/4 cup	60 mL
Corn syrup	1/4 cup	60 mL
Cream of tartar	1/2 tsp.	2 mL
Salt	1/8 tsp.	0.5 mL
Vanilla	1 tsp.	5 mL

Grease side of large heavy saucepan. Combine first 7 ingredients in saucepan. Heat and stir on medium-low to dissolve sugar slowly. Bring to a boil. Brush side of saucepan with damp pastry brush to allow any sugar crystals on side of saucepan to dissolve. Boil slowly, uncovered, without stirring, for about 30 minutes until mixture reaches hard crack stage (about 310°F, 154°C on candy thermometer) or until small amount dropped into very cold water separates into hard, brittle threads. Remove from heat.

Stir in vanilla. Pour into greased 8 × 8 inch (20 × 20 cm) pan. Let stand for 25 minutes. Mark into squares with sharp knife, pressing straight down but not quite through toffee. Break apart once cooled completely. Makes 1 1/4 lbs. (560 g). Breaks into about 64 pieces.

1 piece: 40 Calories; 1 g Total Fat; 16 mg Sodium; trace Protein; 8 g Carbohydrate; 0 g Dietary Fibre

Pictured on page 53.

Pictured on page 53.

Paré Pointer
One good turn deserves another.
Actually, one good turn gives you most of the blankets.

Homemade Chocolate Marshmallows

Kids and adults alike love this fun, fluffy treat!
These melt-in-your-mouth mallows taste like hot chocolate
and marshmallows in one. The ultimate comfort food.

Icing (confectioner's) sugar	1/2 cup	125 mL
Cocoa, sifted if lumpy	1 tbsp.	15 mL
Cornstarch	1/2 cup	125 mL
Cold water	1/3 cup	75 mL
Envelopes of unflavoured gelatin (1/4 oz., 7 g, each)	2	2
Granulated sugar	1 1/2 cups	375 mL
White corn syrup	1/2 cup	125 mL
Cocoa, sifted if lumpy	3 tbsp.	50 mL
Instant coffee granules	1/4 tsp.	1 mL
Water	1/3 cup	75 mL
Vanilla	1/2 tsp.	2 mL

Combine icing sugar, first amount of cocoa and cornstarch in small dish. Line 8 × 8 inch (20 × 20 cm) or 9 × 9 inch (22 × 22 cm) pan with lightly greased foil. Thickly coat bottom and sides of foil with about 2 tbsp. (30 mL) icing sugar mixture. Reserve remaining icing sugar mixture.

Combine cold water and gelatin in large bowl. Set aside.

Heat and stir next 5 ingredients in large saucepan on medium-low until sugar is dissolved. Brush side of saucepan with damp pastry brush to allow any sugar crystals on side of saucepan to dissolve. Increase heat to medium. Boil vigorously, uncovered, for about 4 minutes, without stirring, until mixture reaches soft ball stage (about 240°F, 116°C, on candy thermometer) or until small amount dropped into very cold water forms a soft ball that flattens on its own accord when removed. Do not overcook. Immediately remove from heat. Slowly pour hot syrup into gelatin mixture while beating on medium. Increase speed to high. Beat for about 15 minutes, scraping down side of bowl 2 to 3 times.

(continued on next page)

Candies & Confections

Add vanilla during last few minutes of beating, until mixture is thick and fluffy. Scrape into prepared pan. Spread evenly. Sprinkle with about 2 tbsp. (30 mL) reserved icing sugar mixture. Let stand at room temperature for several hours or overnight until set. Turn out onto work surface. Remove and discard foil. Cut with long greased sharp knife, pushing straight down into marshmallow mixture with full length of blade. Re-grease knife as necessary to make cutting easier. Put remaining icing sugar mixture into shallow dish or on waxed paper. Roll marshmallows to coat completely. Store in airtight container for up to 2 weeks. To serve, tap off excess icing sugar mixture or shake gently in sieve. Makes about 2 dozen marshmallows.

1 marshmallow: 95 Calories; 0.1 g Total Fat; 6 mg Sodium; trace Protein; 24 g Carbohydrate; trace Dietary Fibre

Mints

These delectable little mints are the perfect finale to a special meal. Bite-sized mints with a creamy, melt-in-your-mouth texture. Different shapes can be made by using 1/2 inch (12 mm) pastry or canapé cutters.

Hard margarine (or butter), softened	2 tbsp.	30 mL
Egg white (large)	1	1
Peppermint flavouring	1/2 tsp.	2 mL
Drops of green food colouring	3	3
Icing (confectioner's) sugar, more if needed	2 1/2 cups	625 mL

Beat margarine, egg white, flavouring and food colouring in small bowl.

Slowly beat in icing sugar. Shape into 1/2 inch (12 mm) balls or roll out into 1/4 inch (6 mm) thick rope. Cut into 1/2 inch (12 mm) pieces. Arrange on waxed paper-lined baking sheet. Let stand overnight until dry. Store in airtight container. Makes 13 oz. (370 g). Makes 7 1/2 to 8 dozen mints.

5 mints: 81 Calories; 1.3 g Total Fat; 18 mg Sodium; trace Protein; 18 g Carbohydrate; 0 g Dietary Fibre

Coconut Marshmallow Creams

A surprisingly easy and unusual sweet treat. These tender mallows have a delicious, crispy, sweet coconut coating. Excellent as lunch box treats.

Long thread coconut, toasted (see Tip, page 79)	1 1/2 cups	375 mL
Envelopes of unflavoured gelatin (1/4 oz., 7 g, each)	2	2
Cold water	1/3 cup	75 mL
Granulated sugar	1 1/3 cups	325 mL
White corn syrup	1/2 cup	125 mL
Water	1/3 cup	75 mL
Salt, just a pinch		
Vanilla	1 tsp.	5 mL

Line 8 × 8 inch (20 × 20 cm) pan with lightly greased foil. Sprinkle 1/2 cup (125 mL) coconut over bottom of pan. Reserve remaining coconut.

Sprinkle gelatin over cold water in large bowl. Set aside.

Heat and stir next 4 ingredients in large saucepan on medium until sugar is dissolved. Brush side of saucepan with damp pastry brush to allow any sugar crystals on side of saucepan to dissolve. Increase heat to medium-high. Boil vigorously, uncovered, for about 4 minutes, without stirring, until mixture reaches soft ball stage (about 240°F, 116°C on candy thermometer) or until small amount dropped into very cold water forms a soft ball that flattens on its own accord when removed. Do not overcook. Immediately remove from heat. Slowly pour hot syrup into gelatin mixture while beating on medium. Increase speed to high. Beat for about 15 minutes, scraping down side of bowl 2 to 3 times.

(continued on next page)

Add vanilla during last few minutes of beating, until mixture is thick and fluffy. Scrape into prepared pan. Spread evenly. Sprinkle with 1/2 cup (125 mL) reserved coconut. Let stand at room temperature for several hours or overnight until set. Turn out onto work surface. Remove and discard foil. Cut with long greased sharp knife, pushing straight down into marshmallow mixture with full length of blade. Re-grease knife as necessary to make cutting easier. Put remaining coconut into shallow dish or on waxed paper. Roll marshmallows to coat completely. Store in airtight container for up to 2 weeks. Makes about 2 dozen marshmallows.

1 marshmallow: 96 Calories; 2 g Total Fat; 21 mg Sodium; 1 g Protein; 20 g Carbohydrate; 1 g Dietary Fibre

---

Broken Glass

A rose-coloured, glass-like candy with a tangy berry flavour.
Break into pieces and display in a candy dish.

Granulated sugar	3 3/4 cups	925 mL
Water	1 1/4 cups	300 mL
White corn syrup	1 1/2 cups	375 mL
Cherry (or strawberry) candy flavouring	1/4 tsp.	1 mL
Drops of red food colouring	9	9

Heat and stir sugar, water and corn syrup in large saucepan on medium until boiling and sugar is dissolved. Reduce heat to medium-low. Brush side of saucepan with damp pastry brush to allow any sugar crystals on side of saucepan to dissolve. Boil slowly, without stirring, for 60 to 75 minutes until mixture reaches hard crack stage (about 300°F, 150°C, on candy thermometer) or until small amount dropped into very cold water separates into hard, brittle threads. Remove from heat.

Add candy flavouring and food colouring. Stir. Pour into greased 11 x 17 inch (28 x 43 cm) baking sheet with sides. Let stand for about 45 minutes until cool. Turn out onto cutting board. Break into bite-size pieces. Makes 2 1/2 lbs. (1.1 kg).

1/2 oz. (14 g): 59 Calories; 0 g Total Fat; 5 mg Sodium; 0 g Protein; 15 g Carbohydrate; 0 g Dietary Fibre

Pictured on page 53.

Apricot Pecan Bark

A swirly white and milk chocolate bark with chewy apricots and crunchy pecans. This snack is such fun to make and your guests will marvel at how pretty it is.

Milk chocolate candy bars (3 1/2 oz., 100 g, each), chopped	2	2
Finely chopped dried apricots	1/2 cup	125 mL
White chocolate candy bars (3 1/2 oz., 100 g, each), chopped	2	2
Finely chopped pecans	1/2 cup	125 mL

Heat milk chocolate in heavy medium saucepan on lowest heat for about 5 minutes, stirring often, until almost melted. Do not overheat. Remove from heat. Stir until smooth. Add apricots. Stir.

Heat white chocolate in heavy medium saucepan on lowest heat for about 5 minutes, stirring often, until almost melted. Do not overheat. Remove from heat. Stir until smooth.

Add pecans. Stir. Alternately spoon milk chocolate mixture and white chocolate mixture onto parchment paper-lined 10 × 15 inch (25 × 38 cm) baking sheet. Swirl both mixtures together using wooden skewer. Smooth top. Chill for about 2 hours until set. Break into bite-size pieces. Makes about 1/2 lb. (225 g). Makes about 35 pieces.

1 piece: 76 Calories; 4.7 g Total Fat; 10 mg Sodium; 1 g Protein; 8 g Carbohydrate; trace Dietary Fibre

Pictured on page 72.

Paré Pointer
Disgusted ant to another: "Life is just one big picnic to you."

Mandarin Truffles

A definite must for your holiday baking list! These rich, chocolatey balls
have a festive orange flavour and mild nutty crunch.

Dark chocolate candy bar, chopped	3 1/2 oz.	100 g
Whipping cream	3 tbsp.	50 mL
Orange-flavoured liqueur (such as Grand Marnier)	1 tbsp.	15 mL
Finely chopped pistachios	1/3 cup	75 mL
Finely grated mandarin (or any orange) zest	1 1/2 tsp.	7 mL
Cocoa, sifted if lumpy	2 tbsp.	30 mL

Heat chocolate, whipping cream and liqueur in medium saucepan on
lowest heat for about 3 minutes, stirring often, until almost melted. Do not
overheat. Remove from heat. Stir until smooth.

Add pistachios and mandarin zest. Mix well. Chill for about 1 hour, stirring
occasionally, until firm enough to roll into balls.

Shape rounded teaspoonfuls into balls. Place on foil-lined baking sheet.
Chill for 30 minutes. Place cocoa in shallow dish or on waxed paper. Roll
each ball in cocoa to coat lightly. Chill for 1 to 3 hours until firm. Store in
airtight container for up to 2 weeks. Makes about 18 truffles.

1 truffle: 57 Calories; 4 g Total Fat; 2 mg Sodium; 1 g Protein; 5 g Carbohydrate; 1 g Dietary Fibre

Variation: Omit orange-flavoured liqueur and pistachios. Use same
amounts of coffee-flavoured liqueur (such as Kahlúa) and pecans.

 Store chocolate in a cool, dry place for up to one year. Chocolate
absorbs odours easily, so store in airtight container away from
strong-smelling food.

Crispy Sandwich Cookies

These buttery, crispy oatmeal wafers are scrumptious, both on their own and with the chocolate filling. Serve them filled for a simple, yet rich and elegant, treat.

Hard margarine (or butter), softened	1 cup	250 mL
Granulated sugar	3/4 cup	175 mL
Brown sugar, packed	3/4 cup	175 mL
Large egg	1	1
Vanilla	1 tsp.	5 mL
All-purpose flour	1 1/3 cups	325 mL
Baking soda	3/4 tsp.	4 mL
Salt	1/4 tsp.	1 mL
Coarsely crushed corn flakes cereal	1 1/4 cups	300 mL
Rolled oats (not instant)	1 1/4 cups	300 mL
Medium coconut	2/3 cup	150 mL
CHOCOLATE FILLING		
Semi-sweet chocolate chips	1 cup	250 mL
Icing (confectioner's) sugar	1/2 cup	125 mL
Water	1 tbsp.	15 mL
Block of light cream cheese, softened and cut into pieces	4 oz.	125 g

Cream margarine and both sugars in medium bowl. Beat in egg and vanilla.

Combine flour, baking soda and salt in small bowl. Add to margarine mixture. Mix well.

Add cereal, rolled oats and coconut. Mix. Shape into 1 inch (2.5 cm) balls. Arrange 2 inches (5 cm) apart on greased cookie sheets. Press with fork. Bake in 350°F (175°C) oven for about 15 minutes until golden. Remove to wire racks to cool. Makes about 5 1/2 dozen cookies.

(continued on next page)

Cookies

Chocolate Filling: Heat chocolate chips in small saucepan on lowest heat, stirring often, until almost melted. Do not overheat. Remove from heat. Stir until smooth.

Stir in icing sugar and water. Add cream cheese. Beat on low until smooth. Makes 1 1/4 cups (300 mL) filling. Sandwich cookies together, rough sides facing out, with 2 tsp. (10 mL) filling. Makes about 2 1/2 dozen cookies.

1 cookie: 217 Calories; 10.9 g Total Fat; 203 mg Sodium; 3 g Protein; 29 g Carbohydrate; 1 g Dietary Fibre

Cherry Coconut Macaroons

Wonderfully blended flavours of almond, coconut and cherry in a sweet, chewy macaroon! Almost too pretty to eat—but not quite!

Flake coconut	2 cups	500 mL
Sliced almonds, toasted (see Tip, page 79)	1/2 cup	125 mL
Maraschino cherries, chopped and blotted dry	3/4 cup	175 mL
All-purpose flour	1/2 cup	125 mL
Salt	1/4 tsp.	1 mL
Egg whites (large), room temperature	4	4
Almond flavouring	1/2 tsp.	2 mL
Granulated sugar	1/2 cup	125 mL

Combine first 5 ingredients in medium bowl.

Beat egg whites and flavouring in large bowl on medium until frothy. Add sugar, 1 tbsp. (15 mL) at a time, until soft peaks form. Fold in cherry mixture until just moistened. Drop by spoonfuls, using about 2 tbsp. (30 mL) for each, about 2 inches (5 cm) apart onto greased cookie sheets. Bake in 325°F (160°C) oven for about 15 minutes until edges are golden. Remove to wire racks to cool. Makes about 2 1/2 dozen macaroons.

1 macaroon: 64 Calories; 2.7 g Total Fat; 41 mg Sodium; 1 g Protein; 9 g Carbohydrate; 1 g Dietary Fibre

Pictured on page 54.

Soft Apricot Cashew Chews

The mixture of apricots and nuts gives a wonderful flavour and texture to these golden macaroon-like treats.

Coarsely crushed corn flakes cereal	2 cups	500 mL
Salted cashews, toasted (see Tip, page 79), chopped	3/4 cup	175 mL
Dried apricots, finely chopped	1/2 cup	125 mL
Egg whites (large), room temperature	4	4
Vanilla	1/2 tsp.	2 mL
Icing (confectioner's) sugar	1 cup	250 mL

Combine cereal, cashews and apricots in medium bowl.

Beat egg whites and vanilla in large bowl on high until almost stiff. Add icing sugar, 1/4 cup (60 mL) at a time, until glossy and very soft peaks form. Fold in cereal mixture. Drop by rounded tablespoonfuls about 2 inches (5 cm) apart onto greased cookie sheets. Bake in 325°F (160°C) oven for about 15 minutes until lightly golden. Remove to wire racks to cool. Makes about 2 1/2 dozen cookies.

1 cookie: 67 Calories; 1.4 g Total Fat; 73 mg Sodium; 1 g Protein; 12 g Carbohydrate; trace Dietary Fibre

1. English Toffee, page 43
2. Broken Glass, page 47
3. Spiced Toffee Nuts, page 131
4. Seed And Honey Fruit Plums, page 37

Props Courtesy Of: Wal-Mart Canada Inc.

Orange And Carrot Cookies

Like a fruit and nut health bar in cookie form. A chewy cookie with the pleasing crunch of nuts and hint of zesty orange.

Large egg	1	1
Cooking oil	1/3 cup	75 mL
Brown sugar, packed	1/3 cup	75 mL
Grated carrot	1/2 cup	125 mL
Finely chopped dates	1/3 cup	75 mL
Finely chopped pecans	1/3 cup	75 mL
Freshly squeezed orange juice	1 tbsp.	15 mL
Finely grated orange zest	1 tsp.	5 mL
All-purpose flour	1 cup	250 mL
Baking powder	1 tsp.	5 mL
Salt	1/4 tsp.	1 mL

Combine egg, cooking oil and brown sugar in large bowl.

Add next 5 ingredients. Mix well.

Stir flour, baking powder and salt into carrot mixture. Mix well. Drop by rounded tablespoonfuls about 2 inches (5 cm) apart onto greased cookie sheets. Bake in 350°F (175°C) oven for about 15 minutes until golden. Let stand on cookie sheets for 10 minutes before removing to wire racks to cool. Makes about 1 1/2 dozen cookies.

1 cookie: 111 Calories; 6.2 g Total Fat; 60 mg Sodium; 1 g Protein; 13 g Carbohydrate; 1 g Dietary Fibre

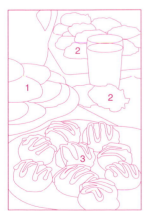

1. Cranberry Chocolate Cookies, page 61
2. Cherry Coconut Macaroons, page 51
3. Pecan Caramel Kisses, page 57

Coffee Meringues

These fancy little meringues are perfect with your after-dinner coffee.
Elegantly dipped in chocolate and delicately flavoured with coffee.

Egg whites (large), room temperature	2	2
Cream of tartar	1/2 tsp.	2 mL
Granulated sugar	1/3 cup	75 mL
Icing (confectioner's) sugar, sifted	1/3 cup	75 mL
Instant coffee granules	1 tbsp.	15 mL
Warm water	1 tbsp.	15 mL
Semi-sweet chocolate baking squares (1 oz., 28 g, each), chopped	4	4

Beat egg whites and cream of tartar in medium bowl on medium until soft peaks form.

Add granulated sugar, 1 tbsp. (15 mL) at a time, until stiff peaks form and sugar is dissolved.

Fold in icing sugar.

Stir coffee granules into warm water in small bowl until dissolved. Fold into meringue. Spoon meringue into piping bag fitted with plain 1 1/2 inch (3.8 cm) nozzle. Pipe about 40 small pointed mounds (about 1/2 inch, 1.2 cm, high and 1 inch, 2.5 cm, in diameter) about 2 inches (5 cm) apart onto greased cookie sheets. Bake on lowest rack in 225°F (110°C) oven for 35 to 40 minutes until dry. Turn oven off. Let meringues stand in oven until cool.

Heat chocolate in medium saucepan on lowest heat, stirring often, until almost melted. Do not overheat. Remove from heat. Stir until smooth. Dip 1/2 of each meringue into chocolate, allowing excess to drip back into saucepan. Place on foil or waxed paper-lined cookie sheets. Let stand in cool place until chocolate is set. Do not chill. Makes about 3 1/2 dozen meringues.

1 meringue: 24 Calories; 0.8 g Total Fat; 3 mg Sodium; trace Protein; 4 g Carbohydrate; trace Dietary Fibre

Pictured on page 107.

Pecan Caramel Kisses

Light and crispy meringues drizzled with a sticky caramel sauce.
Crunchy toasted pecans make this an immensely satisfying sweet treat.

Egg whites (large), room temperature	2	2
Cream of tartar	1/8 tsp.	0.5 mL
Maple flavouring	1/4 tsp.	1 mL
Icing (confectioner's) sugar	1 cup	250 mL
Whole pecans, toasted (see Tip, page 79), finely chopped	1/3 cup	75 mL
Caramels	10	10
Milk	2 tsp.	10 mL

Beat egg whites, cream of tartar and flavouring in medium bowl on medium until stiff peaks form. Beat in icing sugar, 2 tbsp. (30 mL) at a time, until very glossy and stiff.

Fold in pecans. Drop by level tablespoonfuls about 2 inches (5 cm) apart onto greased parchment paper-lined cookie sheets. Bake in 275°F (140°C) oven for about 30 minutes until dry and edges are golden. Remove from parchment paper to wire racks to cool.

Heat and stir caramels and milk in small saucepan on medium-low until smooth. Cool slightly. Spoon into bottom corner of small resealable freezer bag. Snip tiny piece off corner. Drizzle caramel over meringues. Makes about 2 1/2 dozen meringues.

1 meringue: 36 Calories; 1.1 g Total Fat; 10 mg Sodium; trace Protein; 7 g Carbohydrate; trace Dietary Fibre

Pictured on page 54.

Pictured on page 54.

Paré Pointer
The woman covered herself with vanishing cream.
Nobody knows where she went.

Giant Candy Bar Cookies

These cookies often don't make it from the cookie sheet to the cookie jar!
Irresistible when hot from the oven even if they are a little expensive to make.

Hard margarine (or butter), softened	1 cup	250 mL
Granulated sugar	1 cup	250 mL
Brown sugar, packed	1 cup	250 mL
Large eggs, fork-beaten	2	2
Vanilla	2 tsp.	10 mL
All-purpose flour	2 cups	500 mL
Baking powder	1 tsp.	5 mL
Baking soda	1 tsp.	5 mL
Salt	1/2 tsp.	2 mL
Rolled oats (not instant)	2 1/3 cups	575 mL
Chocolate-covered crispy toffee bars (such as Skor or Heath), 1 1/2 oz. (39 g) each, chopped	8	8
Granulated sugar	1/4 cup	60 mL

Cream margarine, first amount of granulated sugar and brown sugar in large bowl. Beat in eggs, 1 at a time, beating well after each addition. Add vanilla. Mix.

Add next 4 ingredients. Stir until just moistened.

Add rolled oats and chocolate bar pieces. Mix well. Shape into 2 inch (5 cm) balls. Arrange 4 or 5 balls on large greased cookie sheet.

Dip bottom of glass into second amount of granulated sugar. Flatten cookies to 1/2 inch (12 mm) thick, dipping glass in sugar as necessary. Bake in 375°F (190°C) oven for about 11 minutes until lightly golden. Let stand on cookie sheet for 5 minutes before removing to wire rack to cool. Repeat with remaining cookie dough. Makes about 3 dozen cookies.

1 cookie: 204 Calories; 9.2 g Total Fat; 168 mg Sodium; 3 g Protein; 29 g Carbohydrate; 1 g Dietary Fibre

Pictured on page 126.

(continued on next page)

Variation: For smaller cookies, shape into 1 1/2 inch (3.8 cm) balls. Arrange about 2 inches (5 cm) apart on greased cookie sheets. Flatten cookies slightly with bottom of glass dipped in second amount of granulated sugar. Bake in 375°F (190°C) oven for 8 to 10 minutes until lightly golden. Makes about 5 dozen cookies.

Anzac Cookies

A sweet treat favourite of the Australian And New Zealand Army Corps.
A satisfying cookie of oats and coconut. Great for dunking in coffee, tea or milk.

Rolled oats (not instant)	1 cup	250 mL
All-purpose flour	1 cup	250 mL
Granulated sugar	1 cup	250 mL
Medium coconut	2/3 cup	150 mL
Hard margarine (or butter), chopped	1/2 cup	125 mL
Cane syrup (such as Rogers)	1 tbsp.	15 mL
Boiling water	2 tbsp.	30 mL
Baking soda	1 tsp.	5 mL

Combine first 4 ingredients in large bowl.

Heat and stir margarine and cane syrup in medium saucepan on medium-low until margarine is melted. Remove from heat.

Mix boiling water and baking soda in small cup. Add to margarine mixture. Mixture will foam a bit. Stir. Add to rolled oat mixture. Mix well. Shape into 1 1/4 inch (3 cm) balls. Arrange about 2 inches (5 cm) apart on greased cookie sheets. Flatten slightly using spatula. Bake in 325°F (160°C) oven for 15 to 20 minutes until golden. Let stand on cookie sheets for 10 minutes before removing to wire racks to cool. Makes about 2 1/2 dozen cookies.

1 cookie: 101 Calories; 4.9 g Total Fat; 82 mg Sodium; 1 g Protein; 14 g Carbohydrate; 1 g Dietary Fibre

Chocolate Malt Cookies

Moist, dark cookies with a rich chocolate flavour.
Give them a fancy look by drizzling with melted white chocolate.

Semi-sweet chocolate baking squares (1 oz., 28 g, each), chopped	8	8
Hard margarine (or butter), cut up	1/2 cup	125 mL
All-purpose flour	1 1/2 cups	375 mL
Baking powder	1/2 tsp.	2 mL
Cocoa, sifted if lumpy	1/2 cup	125 mL
Brown sugar, packed	1 cup	250 mL
Malted milk balls, coarsely chopped	1 cup	250 mL
Large eggs, fork-beaten	2	2

Melt chocolate and margarine in medium saucepan on lowest heat, stirring often, until almost melted. Do not overheat. Remove from heat. Stir until smooth. Cool slightly.

Stir flour, baking powder and cocoa in large bowl.

Add brown sugar and milk balls. Mix well.

Add eggs and chocolate mixture. Stir. Shape into 1 1/4 inch (3 cm) balls. Arrange about 2 inches (5 cm) apart on greased cookie sheets. Bake in 350°F (175°C) oven for about 15 minutes until cooked. Rearrange trays at halftime. Let stand on cookie sheets for 5 minutes before removing to wire racks to cool. Makes about 3 1/2 dozen cookies.

1 cookie: 111 Calories; 5.6 g Total Fat; 38 mg Sodium; 1 g Protein; 16 g Carbohydrate; 1 g Dietary Fibre

---

Paré Pointer
Fleas "itch hike" from dog to dog.

Cookies

Cranberry Chocolate Cookies

Chunky, festive, flavourful cookies perfect for any sweet craving!
Great for a mid-afternoon snack or an energy boost after ball practice.

Large eggs	2	2
Brown sugar, packed	1 2/3 cups	400 mL
Vanilla	1 tsp.	5 mL
All-purpose flour	1 3/4 cups	425 mL
Baking powder	1 tsp.	5 mL
Baking soda	1/2 tsp.	2 mL
Cooking oil	1/2 cup	125 mL
Dried cranberries	1/2 cup	125 mL
Unsalted peanuts	1/2 cup	125 mL
White chocolate chips	1/2 cup	125 mL

Beat eggs, brown sugar and vanilla in large bowl for about 3 minutes until light and creamy.

Stir flour, baking powder and baking soda into egg mixture. Mix well.

Add remaining 4 ingredients. Mix well. Cover. Chill for 1 hour. Shape into balls, using 1 tbsp. (15 mL) for each. Arrange 2 inches (5 cm) apart on greased cookie sheets. Bake in 350°F (175°C) oven for about 15 minutes until golden. Let stand on cookie sheets for 5 minutes before removing to wire racks to cool. Makes about 3 1/2 dozen cookies.

1 cookie: 108 Calories; 4.6 g Total Fat; 33 mg Sodium; 1 g Protein; 16 g Carbohydrate;
1 g Dietary Fibre

Pictured on page 54.

 To save time when baking cookies, you can get the next batch ready on large piece of parchment paper. When one batch comes out of oven, simply slip the parchment paper off the baking sheet and replace it with a new batch.

Lemon Sugar Slices

Buttery sweet crisps with a tang of lemon. Perfect with a cup of tea. Simplicity gives this treat its class.

Butter (not margarine), softened	1/2 cup	125 mL
Granulated sugar	1/2 cup	125 mL
Package of lemon-flavoured jelly powder (gelatin)	3 oz.	85 g
Finely grated lemon peel	2 tsp.	10 mL
Cold water	2 tbsp.	30 mL
All-purpose flour	1 1/2 cups	375 mL
Baking powder	1/2 tsp.	2 mL
Salt	1/4 tsp.	1 mL
Coarse sugar crystals (optional)	2 1/2 tbsp.	37 mL

Cream butter, granulated sugar, jelly powder, lemon peel and cold water in medium bowl.

Mix flour, baking powder and salt in small bowl. Gradually add to butter mixture. Mix until just moistened. Shape into rough log about 2 inches (5 cm) in diameter. Cover with plastic wrap. Roll out into smooth log. Freeze for 30 minutes. Cut into 1/4 inch (6 mm) slices. Lay slices flat, 2 inches (5 cm) apart, on greased cookie sheets.

Sprinkle about 1/8 tsp. (0.5 mL) coarse sugar on each slice. Bake in 350°F (175°C) oven for about 12 minutes until barely coloured on bottom. Remove to wire racks to cool. Makes about 5 dozen cookies.

1 cookie: 39 Calories; 1.7 g Total Fat; 33 mg Sodium; trace Protein; 6 g Carbohydrate; trace Dietary Fibre

Paré Pointer

Young little monsters like to play hide and shriek.

Famous Cookies

The ultimate oatmeal cookie with chocolate chips and nuts.
The perfect energy booster for your active family.

Hard margarine (or butter), softened	3/4 cup	175 mL
Brown sugar, packed	1/2 cup	125 mL
Granulated sugar	1/2 cup	125 mL
Large eggs	2	2
Vanilla	1/2 tsp.	2 mL
All-purpose flour	1 cup	250 mL
Quick-cooking rolled oats (not instant), processed in blender for 10 to 15 seconds	1 1/4 cups	300 mL
Baking powder	1/2 tsp.	2 mL
Baking soda	1/2 tsp.	2 mL
Salt	1/4 tsp.	1 mL
Semi-sweet chocolate chips	1 cup	250 mL
Sweet chocolate baking squares (1 oz., 28 g, each), grated	2	2
Chopped pecans	3/4 cup	175 mL

Cream margarine and both sugars in large bowl. Beat in eggs, 1 at a time, beating well after each addition. Add vanilla. Mix.

Stir next 5 ingredients together in medium bowl. Add to margarine mixture. Mix well.

Add chocolate chips, grated chocolate and pecans. Mix. Shape into 1 1/4 inch (3 cm) balls or drop by spoonfuls 2 inches (5 cm) apart onto well-greased cookie sheets. Bake in 375°F (190°C) oven for about 10 minutes until edges are golden. Remove to wire racks to cool. Makes about 5 dozen cookies.

1 cookie: 84 Calories; 5 g Total Fat; 56 mg Sodium; 1 g Protein; 10 g Carbohydrate; 1 g Dietary Fibre

Mocha Crinkles

These tantalizing cookies are the perfect blend of mocha and chocolate.
Crunchy on the outside and chewy on the inside. One just isn't enough.

Hard margarine (or butter), softened	1/2 cup	125 mL
Brown sugar, packed	1 cup	250 mL
Granulated sugar	3/4 cup	175 mL
Large eggs	3	3
Vanilla	1 1/2 tsp.	7 mL
Unsweetened chocolate baking squares (1 oz., 28 g, each), cut up	2	2
Instant coffee granules, crushed to fine powder	1 tbsp.	15 mL
All-purpose flour	2 cups	500 mL
Baking powder	1 1/2 tsp.	7 mL
Salt	1/2 tsp.	2 mL
Granulated sugar	1/3 cup	75 mL

Cream margarine, brown sugar and first amount of granulated sugar in large bowl. Beat in eggs, 1 at a time, beating well after each addition. Add vanilla. Mix.

Heat chocolate and coffee granules in small saucepan on lowest heat, stirring often, until almost melted. Do not overheat. Remove from heat. Stir until smooth. Add to margarine mixture. Mix well.

Stir in flour, baking powder and salt. Cover. Chill for at least 2 hours or overnight. Shape into 1 1/4 inch (3 cm) balls.

Put second amount of granulated sugar into shallow dish or on waxed paper. Roll balls in sugar to coat completely. Arrange 2 inches (5 cm) apart on greased cookie sheets. Bake in 350°F (175°C) oven for 10 to 12 minutes until slightly puffy and have cracked appearance on top. Do not overbake. Cookies will be soft. Remove to wire racks to cool. Makes about 3 1/2 dozen cookies.

1 cookie: 98 Calories; 3.5 g Total Fat; 75 mg Sodium; 1 g Protein; 16 g Carbohydrate; trace Dietary Fibre

Crunch Cheesecake

Who ever said cheesecake had to be difficult to prepare? This chilled sweet treat is so rich, creamy and easy to make that you'll prepare it again and again.

Chocolate wafer crumbs	2 cups	500 mL
Hard margarine (or butter), melted	2/3 cup	150 mL
FILLING		
Envelope of unflavoured gelatin	1/4 oz.	7 g
Cold water	1/4 cup	60 mL
Blocks of cream cheese (8 oz., 250 g, each), softened	2	2
Granulated sugar	1/2 cup	125 mL
Vanilla	1 tsp.	5 mL
Whipping cream	1/2 cup	125 mL
Chocolate-covered sponge toffee candy bars (such as Crunchie), 1 1/2 oz. (44 g) each, chopped	5	5
Cocoa, for dusting		

Combine wafer crumbs and margarine in medium bowl until well mixed. Pack into bottom and up side of ungreased 9 inch (22 cm) springform pan. Chill for 1 hour.

Filling: Sprinkle gelatin over water in small saucepan. Let stand for 1 minute. Heat and stir on medium until gelatin is dissolved. Cool.

Beat next 4 ingredients in large bowl until smooth.

Fold in chopped candy bar and gelatin mixture. Turn into crust. Spread evenly. Cover. Chill overnight.

Dust with cocoa. Cuts into 12 wedges.

1 wedge: 486 Calories; 36.3 g Total Fat; 380 mg Sodium; 6 g Protein; 36 g Carbohydrate; trace Dietary Fibre

Cherry Oat Dessert

The golden brown crumble and the rich cherry red filling will delight your guests.
Makes a delicious dessert when served hot but is
also good as a cold small square.

CRUST		
White cake mix (2 layer size)	1	1
Rolled oats (not instant)	1 cup	250 mL
Hard margarine (or butter), chilled	1/2 cup	125 mL
Large egg	1	1
Can of cherry pie filling	19 oz.	540 mL
Chopped pecans	3/4 cup	175 mL
Brown sugar, packed	1/3 cup	75 mL
Rolled oats (not instant)	1/4 cup	60 mL
Hard margarine (or butter)	2 tbsp.	30 mL

Crust: Stir cake mix and first amount of rolled oats together. Cut in first amount of margarine until coarse crumbs form. Reserve 1 2/3 cups (400 mL).

Add egg to remaining oat mixture. Stir. Pack into greased 9 x 13 inch (22 x 33 cm) pan using sheet of waxed paper to press down in even layer.

Spread pie filling over oat mixture.

Combine reserved oat mixture, pecans, brown sugar and second amount of rolled oats in medium bowl. Cut in second amount of margarine until coarse crumbs form. Sprinkle over pie filling. Bake in 350°F (175°C) oven for 50 to 60 minutes until golden. Let stand for 10 minutes to cool slightly. Cuts into 12 pieces.

1 piece: 456 Calories; 21.2 g Total Fat; 419 mg Sodium; 5 g Protein; 64 g Carbohydrate; 2 g Dietary Fibre

CHERRY OAT BITES: Chill. Cut into 54 squares.

Sweet Banana Packets

These unique treats are as much fun to prepare as they are to eat.
Ideal for birthday parties. What kid doesn't love bananas,
chocolate, marshmallows and ice cream?

Ripe medium bananas	2	2
Lemon juice	1 tbsp.	15 mL
Large flour tortillas (about 10 inches, 25 cm)	4	4
Miniature marshmallows	1/2 cup	125 mL
Milk chocolate candy bar, coarsely chopped	3 1/2 oz.	100 g
Brown sugar, packed	2 tbsp.	30 mL
Ground cinnamon	1/4 tsp.	1 mL
Hard margarine (or butter), melted	2 tbsp.	30 mL
Caramel ice cream topping	1/4 cup	60 mL
Scoops of vanilla ice cream (optional)	4	4

Cut each banana in half lengthwise and then crosswise, for a total of 8 pieces. Brush with lemon juice.

Place 2 banana pieces on each tortilla to 1 side of centre. Divide and sprinkle marshmallows and chocolate over each.

Combine brown sugar and cinnamon in small bowl. Sprinkle about 1 tsp. (5 mL) over chocolate on each tortilla. Reserve remaining brown sugar mixture. Roll up tortillas, while tucking in sides to enclose filling. Arrange, seam-side down, on greased baking sheet.

Brush packets with margarine. Sprinkle with reserved brown sugar mixture. Bake in 425°F (220°C) oven for about 10 minutes until lightly browned and crisp.

Drizzle individual packets with ice cream topping. Serve each with 1 scoop of ice cream. Makes 4 packets.

1 packet: 468 Calories; 16.8 g Total Fat; 368 mg Sodium; 6 g Protein; 78 g Carbohydrate; 3 g Dietary Fibre

Pictured on page 71.

Tropical Rumba Cheesecake

A medley of tropical flavours—coconut, pineapple, maraschino cherries and rum. Exotic-looking, but easy to prepare.

COCONUT COOKIE CRUST		
Coconut cream-filled cookies	13	13
Hard margarine (or butter), melted	3 tbsp.	50 mL
PINEAPPLE FILLING		
Can of crushed pineapple, with juice	14 oz.	398 mL
Instant banana cream pudding powder (4 serving size)	1	1
Icing (confectioner's) sugar	1/4 cup	60 mL
Blocks of light (or regular) cream cheese (8 oz., 250 g, each), softened and cut into 8 pieces each (see Note)	2	2
Whipping cream	1 cup	250 mL
PINEAPPLE RUM SYRUP		
Reserved pineapple juice	1/4 cup	60 mL
Dark (or amber) rum (or 1 tsp., 5 mL, rum flavouring plus water)	1/4 cup	60 mL
Brown sugar, packed	2/3 cup	150 mL
Golden corn syrup	2/3 cup	150 mL
Hard margarine (or butter)	2 tbsp.	30 mL
Maraschino cherries	2/3 cup	150 mL
Can of pineapple tidbits, drained and juice reserved	8 oz.	227 mL

Coconut Cookie Crust: Process cookies in food processor until consistency of fine crumbs. Add margarine. Pulse with on/off motion until mixed. Pack into bottom of ungreased 9 inch (22 cm) springform pan.

Pineapple Filling: Put crushed pineapple with juice, pudding powder, icing sugar and cream cheese into same food processor. Pulse with on/off motion until just mixed. Process until cream cheese is smooth. Turn out into large bowl.

(continued on next page)

Desserts

Beat whipping cream in small bowl until soft peaks form. Fold into cream cheese mixture. Turn out onto crust. Spread evenly. Chill for at least 8 hours or overnight before cutting. Cuts into 12 wedges.

Pineapple Rum Syrup: Combine reserved pineapple juice and rum in medium saucepan. Bring to a boil on medium. Add brown sugar and corn syrup. Heat and stir until brown sugar is dissolved. Boil for about 5 minutes, stirring occasionally, until syrupy. Remove from heat.

Stir in margarine, cherries and pineapple tidbits. Cool to room temperature. Stir. Makes 2 cups (500 mL) syrup. Spoon about 2 1/2 tbsp. (37 mL) over each wedge. Serves 12.

1 serving: 468 Calories; 22 g Total Fat; 615 mg Sodium; 5 g Protein; 63 g Carbohydrate; 1 g Dietary Fibre

Pictured on front cover.

Note: This dessert works well using light cream cheese, reducing the amount of fat in each serving!

Amaretto Strawberries

A very classy dessert prepared in just minutes. A smooth, creamy sauce over fresh, juicy strawberries. Serve in crystal dishes for an elegant light dessert.

Sliced fresh strawberries	1 1/2 cups	375 mL
Icing (confectioner's) sugar	1 1/2 tbsp.	25 mL
Sour cream	1/3 cup	75 mL
Almond-flavoured liqueur (such as Amaretto)	1 tbsp.	15 mL

Put strawberries and icing sugar into medium bowl. Stir. Let stand for about 1 hour until juices form. Drain juice into small bowl.

Add sour cream and liqueur to juice. Stir. Divide and spoon berries into 2 sherbet dishes or fruit nappies. Spoon juice mixture over top. Serves 2.

1 serving: 155 Calories; 6.2 g Total Fat; 19 mg Sodium; 2 g Protein; 20 g Carbohydrate; 3 g Dietary Fibre

Pictured on page 89.

Bowl-O-Bananas

A decadent, hot chocolatey sauce spooned over bananas. Top with a
dollop of whipped dessert topping or add a scoop of ice cream. Or both!

CHOCOLATE SAUCE

Brown sugar, packed	1 cup	250 mL
Cocoa, sifted if lumpy	2 tbsp.	30 mL
Hard margarine (or butter)	1 tbsp.	15 mL
Corn syrup	1 tbsp.	15 mL
Milk	2 tbsp.	30 mL
Vanilla	1/4 tsp.	1 mL
Medium bananas, sliced	4	4
Frozen whipped topping, thawed	1 cup	250 mL

Chocolate Sauce: Put first 6 ingredients into medium saucepan. Heat and
stir on medium until boiling. Gently boil for about 3 minutes, stirring
constantly, until slightly thickened. Makes 3/4 cup (175 mL) sauce.

Divide banana among 4 individual bowls. Divide and spoon sauce over
each.

Top each with whipped topping. Serves 4.

1 serving: 439 Calories; 8.9 g Total Fat; 71 mg Sodium; 2 g Protein; 94 g Carbohydrate;
3 g Dietary Fibre

1. Sweet Banana Packets, page 67
2. Cream-Layered Pastries, page 91

Gooey Banana Fix

When you need a sweet treat that is indulgent, decadent, sweet and fast, prepare this chocolatey, gooey, sticky, lip-smacking treat in just minutes.

Medium banana, sliced lengthwise	1	1
Milk chocolate candy bar (3 1/2 oz., 100 g, size), chopped	1/2	1/2
Caramel ice cream topping	2 tbsp.	30 mL
Miniature marshmallows	16	16

Form oval "dish" from foil, scrunching up sides slightly. Place on ungreased baking sheet. Arrange banana halves in foil, cut side up.

Sprinkle chocolate over banana halves. Drizzle with 1/2 of ice cream topping.

Randomly place marshmallows over top. Drizzle with remaining ice cream topping. Bake in 425°F (220°C) oven for 5 to 6 minutes until marshmallows are puffed and golden and chocolate is almost melted. Cut each piece into thirds. Serves 1 or 2.

1 serving: 485 Calories; 16 g Total Fat; 190 mg Sodium; 5 g Protein; 89 g Carbohydrate; 4 g Dietary Fibre

Variation: Instead of foil, use ovenproof oval dish.

Pictured on page 72.

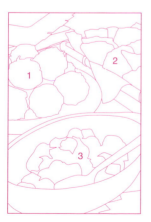

1. Chocolate Banana Snack, page 123
2. Apricot Pecan Bark, page 48
3. Gooey Banana Fix, above

Crown Jewel Dessert

*As pretty as its name! This colourful and fun dessert is
perfect for special occasions such as a sweet 16 birthday party.*

CRUST

Hard margarine (or butter)	1/3 cup	75 mL
Graham cracker crumbs	1 3/4 cups	425 mL
Cocoa, sifted if lumpy	1 tbsp.	15 mL
Package of raspberry-flavoured jelly powder (gelatin)	3 oz.	85 g
Package of orange-flavoured jelly powder (gelatin)	3 oz.	85 g
Package of lime-flavoured jelly powder (gelatin)	3 oz.	85 g
Boiling water	4 1/2 cups	1.1 L
Pineapple juice	1 cup	250 mL
Package of lemon-flavoured jelly powder (gelatin)	3 oz.	85 g
Cold water	1/4 cup	60 mL
Envelopes of dessert topping (prepared), see Note	2	2

Crust: Melt margarine in small saucepan. Stir in graham crumbs and cocoa until well combined. Pack in bottom of ungreased 9 × 13 inch (22 × 33 cm) pan. Bake in 350°F (175°C) oven for 10 minutes. Cool.

Dissolve first 3 amounts of jelly powder in 1 1/2 cups (375 mL) boiling water each in 3 separate bowls. Pour into 3 square pans. Chill until set. Cut into 1/2 inch (12 mm) cubes.

Bring pineapple juice to a boil in small saucepan. Stir in lemon jelly powder until dissolved. Stir in cold water. Chill for about 1 hour, stirring once or twice, until slightly thickened.

Fold lemon jelly powder mixture into dessert topping. Add cubed gelatin mixture using straight-edged lifter to remove from pan. Fold in. Turn into crust. Spread evenly. Chill overnight. Cuts into 18 squares.

1 square: 185 Calories; 6.8 g Total Fat; 155 mg Sodium; 3 g Protein; 29 g Carbohydrate; trace Dietary Fibre

Note: To use whipping cream, beat 2 cups (500 mL) whipping cream and 1/4 cup (60 mL) granulated sugar in medium bowl until soft peaks form.

Sweet Crêpe Roll-Ups

These delicate and easy-to-prepare crêpes are so versatile.
Use with your favourite sweet filling and serve for brunch or
evening dessert. Very European and very chic!

Large eggs	2	2
All-purpose flour	1/2 cup	125 mL
Granulated sugar	1 tsp.	5 mL
Salt	1/4 tsp.	1 mL
Milk	2/3 cup	150 mL
Hard margarine (or butter), melted	2 tbsp.	30 mL
Vanilla	1/2 tsp.	2 mL
Jam, your choice	1/3 cup	75 mL
Icing (confectioner's) sugar, for dusting	2 tsp.	10 mL

Measure first 7 ingredients into small bowl. Beat on low for 1 minute. Stir until air bubbles disappear and mixture is smooth. Heat 7 or 8 inch (18 or 20 cm) greased non-stick frying pan or crêpe pan on medium until hot. Add about 2 tbsp. (30 mL) batter, quickly tilting pan to coat bottom. Cook for 1 to 2 minutes until edges start to brown and top loses shine. Remove to waxed paper to cool. Repeat with remaining batter. Stack cooked crêpes on top of one another.

Spread 1 1/2 to 2 tsp. (7 to 10 mL) jam down centre on unbrowned side of each crêpe. Roll up tightly, jelly roll-style. Arrange in single layer, seam-side down, on serving plate.

Dust with icing sugar. Makes about 10 roll-ups.

1 roll-up: 96 Calories; 3.6 g Total Fat; 112 mg Sodium; 3 g Protein; 14 g Carbohydrate; trace Dietary Fibre

Variation: Omit jam. Use same amount of jelly, chocolate hazelnut spread, peanut butter or lemon spread.

Mango Macadamia Sandwich

Mango and macadamia nuts give this ice cream sandwich a wonderful, tropical taste. The satisfying crunch of nuts gives it a delightful texture. You'll have lots of offers to help you make these fun treats.

All-purpose flour	1 1/2 cups	375 mL
Icing (confectioner's) sugar	3/4 cup	175 mL
Ground cinnamon	3/4 tsp.	4 mL
Finely grated orange zest	2 tsp.	10 mL
Vanilla	1 tsp.	5 mL
Hard margarine (or butter)	1/2 cup	125 mL
Egg yolks (large)	2	2
Vanilla ice cream, softened	2 cups	500 mL
Can of mango slices, drained, chopped	14 oz.	398 mL
Macadamia nuts, toasted (see Tip, page 79), chopped	1/2 cup	125 mL

Put first 5 ingredients into large bowl. Cut in margarine until crumbly.

Add egg yolks. Process until mixture forms ball. Roll out on lightly floured surface (or on lightly floured parchment paper) to 1/4 inch (6 mm) thickness. Cut out using 3 inch (7.5 cm) round fluted cookie cutter. Arrange about 1 inch (2.5 cm) apart on lightly greased cookie sheets. Bake in 350°F (175°C) oven for 10 to 15 minutes until golden. Let stand on cookie sheets for 5 minutes before removing to wire racks to cool. Makes 16 cookies.

Combine ice cream, mango and macadamia nuts in medium bowl. Line 9 x 9 inch (22 x 22 cm) pan with waxed paper, ensuring paper comes up two opposing sides by 2 inches (5 cm). Turn ice cream mixture into pan. Spread evenly. Cover. Freeze for at least 1 hour until firm. Using extended paper on sides of pan, lift ice cream from pan. Cut out rounds, using 2 1/2 inch (6.4 cm) round cookie cutter, as close to each other as possible. Place 1 ice cream round on 1 cookie. Cover with another cookie. Repeat with remaining cookies and ice cream rounds. Return to freezer. Makes 8 sandwiches.

1 sandwich: 400 Calories; 22.9 g Total Fat; 173 mg Sodium; 5 g Protein; 45 g Carbohydrate; 2 g Dietary Fibre

Pictured on page 90.

Berry Ice Cream Cups

Few flavours combine as well as berries and vanilla ice cream.
Add a chocolatey crust and a berry juice sauce and you have perfection.
Keep these delectable little cups in your freezer to surprise guests
and family when their sweet cravings strike.

Chocolate wafers	12	12
Extra-large paper cupcake liners	12	12
Vanilla ice cream, slightly softened	4 cups	1 L
Chopped frozen whole strawberries (or raspberries), thawed, well drained and juice reserved	1 1/2 cups	375 mL
SAUCE		
White corn syrup	1 tbsp.	15 mL
Reserved strawberry juice	3 tbsp.	50 mL

Put wafers into bottom of paper liners set in muffin cups.

Mix ice cream and strawberries in large bowl. Makes 4 cups (1 L) ice cream mixture. Freeze for about 1 hour until slightly firm.

Sauce: Combine corn syrup and reserved juice in small bowl. Makes 1/4 cup (60 mL) sauce. Set aside. Scoop about 1/3 cup (75 mL) ice cream mixture onto each wafer. Spoon 1 tsp. (5 mL) sauce over ice cream in each cup. Swirl to make fancy design. Freeze until solid. Remove from freezer 10 minutes before serving. Makes 12 ice cream cups.

1 ice cream cup: 138 Calories; 6 g Total Fat; 74 mg Sodium; 2 g Protein; 20 g Carbohydrate; 1 g Dietary Fibre

---

Paré Pointer
A tired cow moos badly. An angry crowd boos madly.

Frozen Cheesecake Bites

A creamy lemon cheesecake on a buttery shortbread base. The hint of almond adds a touch of sophistication. Easy to eat by hand straight out of the freezer.

CRUST

All-purpose flour	1 1/2 cups	375 mL
Icing (confectioner's) sugar	2 tbsp.	30 mL
Sliced almonds	3/4 cup	175 mL
Hard margarine (or butter), chilled and cut into pieces	1/2 cup	125 mL
Blocks of cream cheese (8 oz., 250 g, each), softened	2	2
Granulated sugar	1/2 cup	125 mL
Large eggs	2	2
Finely grated lemon zest	1 tbsp.	15 mL
Container of lemon yogurt	6 oz.	175 mL
Cream of wheat	2 tbsp.	30 mL
Vanilla	1/2 tsp.	2 mL
Sliced almonds, toasted (see Tip, page 79), optional	1/4 cup	60 mL

Crust: Put first 3 ingredients into medium bowl. Cut in margarine until crumbly. Press firmly into greased 9 × 13 inch (22 × 33 cm) pan. Bake in 350°F (175°C) oven for 10 minutes.

Beat next 7 ingredients in medium bowl until smooth. Spread over crust.

Sprinkle with second amount of almonds. Bake in 350°F (175°C) oven for 25 to 30 minutes until firmly set and edges are slightly golden. Cool completely. Cut with wet knife into triangles. Arrange 1/2 inch (12 mm) apart on large baking sheet. Freeze for 2 to 3 hours until firm. Store in resealable freezer bags or tins, separating layers with waxed paper. Keep frozen. Cuts into 30 cheesecake bites.

1 cheesecake bite: 157 Calories; 11 g Total Fat; 90 mg Sodium; 3 g Protein; 12 g Carbohydrate; 1 g Dietary Fibre

Pictured on page 125.

Espresso Sundae

Satisfy your coffee, chocolate and ice cream cravings all at once!
Get your favourite spoon and enjoy.

CHOCOLATE DRIZZLE

Whipping cream	1/3 cup	75 mL
Prepared strong coffee	1 tbsp.	15 mL
Semi-sweet chocolate baking squares (1 oz., 28 g, each), chopped	5	5
Hard margarine (or butter)	1 tbsp.	15 mL
Scoops of chocolate ice cream (about 4 cups, 1 L)	16	16
Irish cream-flavoured liqueur (such as Baileys)	1/2 cup	125 mL
Pecans, toasted (see Tip, below), coarsely chopped	1/4 cup	60 mL

Chocolate Drizzle: Combine first 4 ingredients in small saucepan. Heat and stir on low for 3 to 4 minutes until chocolate is melted. Do not overheat. Remove from heat. Cool slightly. Makes about 1 cup (250 mL) Chocolate Drizzle.

Spoon 2 scoops of ice cream each into 8 individual sundae glasses.

Drizzle each with 1 tbsp. (15 mL) liqueur. Drizzle each with 2 tbsp. (30 mL) Chocolate Drizzle. Sprinkle with pecans. Serves 8.

1 serving: 284 Calories; 19.2 g Total Fat; 64 mg Sodium; 3 g Protein; 27 g Carbohydrate; 1 g Dietary Fibre

Pictured on page 107.

 To toast almonds, cashews, coconut, hazelnuts, macadamia nuts and pecans, place in single layer in ungreased shallow pan. Bake in 350°F (175°C) oven for 5 to 10 minutes, stirring or shaking often, until desired doneness.

Chocolate Raspberry Pie

A chocolate ice cream pie with two succulent layers of juicy red raspberries.
Preparation requires a little patience, but tastes all the sweeter for the wait.

COOKIE CRUST

Hard margarine (or butter)	1/3 cup	75 mL
Vanilla wafer crumbs	1 1/4 cups	300 mL

FILLING

Frozen raspberries in syrup, thawed	15 oz.	425 g
Cornstarch	1 tbsp.	15 mL
Chocolate ice cream, softened	3 cups	750 mL
Whipped cream (or prepared dessert topping)	1 1/2 cups	375 mL
Chocolate sauce	1 tbsp.	15 mL

Cookie Crust: Melt margarine in medium saucepan. Add wafer crumbs. Stir until well mixed. Pack into bottom and up side of 9 inch (22 cm) pie plate. Freeze.

Filling: Drain raspberry syrup into small saucepan. Reserve raspberries. Stir cornstarch into syrup. Heat and stir on medium for 6 to 7 minutes until boiling and thickened. Remove from heat. Add reserved raspberries. Chill.

Spoon 1/2 of ice cream into crust. Spread evenly. Spread 1/2 of raspberry mixture over ice cream. Freeze until firm. Spoon remaining ice cream onto frozen raspberry mixture. Spread evenly. Spread remaining raspberry mixture over ice cream. Freeze until firm.

Top with whipped cream. Drizzle with chocolate sauce. Freeze for at least 8 hours or overnight. Cuts into 8 wedges.

1 wedge: 378 Calories; 23.5 g Total Fat; 186 mg Sodium; 4 g Protein; 42 g Carbohydrate; 2 g Dietary Fibre

Pictured on page 90.

Frozen Desserts

Cran-Raspberry Ice

A creamy, iced treat with the summery sweet taste of raspberries and the crisp tartness of cranberries. Your guests will love the frosted rosy colour. A perfect way to beat the heat.

Boiling water	1/2 cup	125 mL
Package of raspberry-flavoured jelly powder (gelatin)	3 oz.	85 g
Frozen whole raspberries, partially thawed	2 1/4 cups	550 mL
Block of cream cheese, softened	4 oz.	125 g
Icing (confectioner's) sugar	1/4 cup	60 mL
Sour cream	1 cup	250 mL
Whole cranberry sauce	14 oz.	398 mL

Add boiling water to jelly powder in small bowl. Stir to dissolve. Stir in raspberries. Set aside.

Beat cream cheese and icing sugar in medium bowl until smooth. Add sour cream and cranberry sauce. Mix. Add raspberry mixture. Stir until well combined. Pour into 1/2 to 3/4 cup (125 to 175 mL) individual molds or 5 cup (1.25 L) freezing mold (see Tip, below). Freeze until firm. Cover. Keep frozen. Serves 10.

1 serving: 256 Calories; 7.9 g Total Fat; 83 mg Sodium; 3 g Protein; 46 g Carbohydrate; 3 g Dietary Fibre

Pictured on page 90.

 Frozen desserts can be set in a variety of containers if you don't have a mold. Line a loaf pan or muffin cups with plastic wrap and fill. If using a mold, the plastic ones are the easiest from which to remove the dessert.

Peanut Ice Cream Treat

Perfect in its simplicity. Vanilla ice cream drizzled with chocolate and caramel and topped with crunchy peanuts. The chocolate wafer crust oozes when cut.

Thick butterscotch (or caramel) ice cream topping	1/3 cup	75 mL
Thick chocolate (or fudge) ice cream topping	1/3 cup	75 mL
Commercial chocolate crumb crust (9 inch, 22 cm, size)	1	1
Vanilla (or butterscotch ripple) ice cream, softened	4 cups	1 L
Dry-roasted peanuts, chopped	1/2 cup	125 mL
Thick butterscotch (or caramel) ice cream topping, for garnish		
Thick chocolate (or fudge) ice cream topping, for garnish		

Spoon first amounts of butterscotch and chocolate toppings, in dabs, into bottom of crust. Freeze for 20 minutes.

Spoon ice cream into crust. Pack evenly to fill in all spaces.

Sprinkle with peanuts. Cover with plastic wrap. Freeze for several hours until firm.

Put second amounts of butterscotch and chocolate toppings into individual small resealable freezer bags. Snip tiny piece off corner. Drizzle over peanuts in lattice design. Freeze. Cuts into 8 wedges.

1 wedge: 413 Calories; 22.1 g Total Fat; 313 mg Sodium; 7 g Protein; 51 g Carbohydrate; 1 g Dietary Fibre

Pictured on page 89.

Jack Frost Lemon Pie

A refreshing chilled dessert that is both sweet and pleasingly tart.
The lemony flavour is perfect for cleansing the palate after a rich meal.
Very welcome on a hot summer day.

Granulated sugar	3/4 cup	175 mL
All-purpose flour	1 tsp.	5 mL
Large egg	1	1
Freshly squeezed lemon juice (about 1 medium lemon)	1/3 cup	75 mL
Finely grated lemon zest	1 tsp.	5 mL
Ground mace	3/4 tsp.	4 mL
Envelope of dessert topping (not prepared)	1	1
Cold milk	1/2 cup	125 mL
Graham cracker crust (9 inch, 22 cm, size)	1	1

Stir sugar and flour in small saucepan. Mix in egg, lemon juice and zest. Heat and stir on medium for about 5 minutes until boiling and thickened. Remove from heat. Cool completely.

Stir in mace.

Stir dessert topping and milk in small bowl. Beat until stiff peaks form. Fold into lemon mixture.

Turn into crust. Freeze until firm. Cuts into 8 wedges.

1 wedge: 276 Calories; 10.4 g Total Fat; 194 mg Sodium; 3 g Protein; 44 g Carbohydrate; trace Dietary Fibre

Paré Pointer
If you have a bad toothache in the rain,
one is roaring with pain, the other is pouring with rain.

Peanut Butter Meringue Pie

A rich, sweet peanut buttery custard pie crowned with soft golden peaks of meringue. A peanut butter lover's delight.

Icing (confectioner's) sugar	2/3 cup	150 mL
Smooth peanut butter	1/3 cup	75 mL
Baked 9 inch (22 cm) pie shell	1	1
Milk	1 3/4 cups	425 mL
All-purpose flour	3 tbsp.	50 mL
Cornstarch	3 tbsp.	50 mL
Granulated sugar	1/2 cup	125 mL
Salt	1/2 tsp.	2 mL
Milk	1/2 cup	125 mL
Egg yolks (large)	3	3
Smooth peanut butter	1/4 cup	60 mL
Vanilla	1 1/2 tsp.	7 mL
MERINGUE		
Egg whites (large), room temperature	3	3
Cream of tartar	1/4 tsp.	1 mL
Cornstarch	1 tsp.	5 mL
Granulated sugar	6 tbsp.	100 mL
Finely chopped peanuts (optional)	1 tbsp.	15 mL

Mix icing sugar and first amount of peanut butter in medium bowl. Work with fingers until consistency of coarse crumbs.

Sprinkle over bottom of pie crust.

Heat first amount of milk in heavy medium saucepan on medium until hot. Do not boil.

Combine flour, cornstarch, granulated sugar and salt in small bowl. Add second amount of milk. Mix until smooth. Stir into hot milk in saucepan until boiling and thickened. Remove from heat.

Beat egg yolks with fork in separate small bowl. Add 1/2 cup (125 mL) hot milk mixture to egg yolks. Mix well. Stir into milk mixture. Heat and stir on medium-low for 2 to 3 minutes until mixture is thickened.

(continued on next page)

Pies & Pastries

Add second amount of peanut butter and vanilla. Stir. Pour over icing sugar mixture in pie crust.

Meringue: Beat egg whites, cream of tartar and cornstarch in medium bowl until almost stiff. Add sugar, 1 tbsp. (15 mL) at a time, until stiff peaks form and sugar is dissolved. Spoon over top of hot filling, sealing edges to crust.

Sprinkle with peanuts. Bake in 350°F (175°C) oven for 10 to 15 minutes until golden. Cuts into 8 wedges.

1 wedge: 413 Calories; 18 g Total Fat; 404 mg Sodium; 11 g Protein; 54 g Carbohydrate; 1 g Dietary Fibre

Nutty Chocolate Pie

This incredible chocolate pie will draw breaths of amazement. So rich, nutty and chocolatey. A small slice will satisfy even the largest sweet craving.

Large eggs	2	2
Brown sugar, packed	1 cup	250 mL
Hard margarine (or butter), melted	3/4 cup	175 mL
Semi-sweet chocolate chips	1 cup	250 mL
Chopped walnuts (or pecans)	3/4 cup	175 mL
Unbaked 9 inch (22 cm) pie shell	1	1

Beat eggs until frothy. Add brown sugar and margarine. Beat until well mixed. Add chocolate chips and walnuts. Stir until well mixed.

Turn into pie shell. Bake on bottom rack in 325°F (160°C) oven for 50 to 60 minutes until wooden pick inserted in centre comes out clean. Cuts into 8 wedges.

1 wedge: 553 Calories; 38.3 g Total Fat; 345 mg Sodium; 6 g Protein; 52 g Carbohydrate; 2 g Dietary Fibre

Pastry Triangles With Pears

A sophisticated, yet easy-to-prepare dessert. Caramelized pears in spiced syrup and rum, nestled in a crispy, flaky puff pastry.

Package of frozen puff pastry (14 oz., 397 g, size), thawed according to package directions	1/2	1/2
Egg yolk (large), fork-beaten	1	1
Sliced almonds	1/4 cup	60 mL
CARAMELIZED PEARS		
Hard margarine (or butter)	1/3 cup	75 mL
Firm medium pears (about 1 1/2 lbs., 680 g), peeled, sliced 1/8 inch (3 mm) thick	4	4
Brown sugar, packed	1/4 cup	60 mL
Maple syrup	2 tbsp.	30 mL
Dark rum (or 1/2 tsp., 2 mL, rum flavouring plus water)	2 tbsp.	30 mL
Ground cinnamon	3/4 tsp.	4 mL
Icing (confectioner's) sugar, for garnish		
Whipped cream, for garnish		

Roll out pastry on lightly floured surface to about 8 × 8 inch (20 × 20 cm) square. Cut into quarters. Cut each quarter into 2 triangles. Arrange about 1/2 inch (12 mm) apart on ungreased baking sheet.

Brush with egg yolk. Sprinkle with almonds. Bake in 400°F (205°C) oven for about 15 minutes until golden. Let stand on baking sheet for 5 minutes before removing to wire rack to cool.

Caramelized Pears: Melt margarine in large frying pan on medium-low. Add next 5 ingredients. Heat and stir for 10 to 15 minutes until pears are soft and sauce is thickened. Split each triangle in half horizontally into 2 layers. Place bottom half of 1 triangle on individual serving plate. Top with 1/8 of pear mixture. Cover with top half of triangle. Repeat with remaining triangles and pear mixture.

Sprinkle with icing sugar. Serve with dollop of whipped cream. Serves 8.

1 serving: 308 Calories; 20 g Total Fat; 162 mg Sodium; 3 g Protein; 29 g Carbohydrate; 2 g Dietary Fibre

Pictured on page 108 and on back cover.

Pies & Pastries

Spiced Palmiers

Pronounced pahlm-YAY. No pastry lover can resist these crispy,
golden treats spiced with cinnamon, ginger and cloves.
The perfect treat to serve when unexpected guests arrive.

Package of frozen puff pastry, thawed according to package directions	14 oz.	397 g
Hard margarine (or butter), melted	2 tbsp.	30 mL
Granulated sugar	1/4 cup	60 mL
Ground cinnamon	1/2 tsp.	2 mL
Ground ginger	1/2 tsp.	2 mL
Ground cloves	1/4 tsp.	1 mL

Roll out pastry on lightly floured surface to about 8 x 14 inch (20 x 35 cm) rectangle.

Brush pastry with margarine.

Combine next 4 ingredients in small bowl. Sprinkle 3 tbsp. (50 mL) over pastry. Fold long sides of pastry in to meet in centre. Brush with margarine. Sprinkle with remaining sugar mixture. Fold in half lengthwise. Press lightly. Cover. Chill for 30 minutes. Cut pastry into 1/2 inch (12 mm) slices. Arrange, cut side down, about 3 inches (7.5 cm) apart on lightly greased baking sheets. Bake in 375°F (190°C) oven for about 20 minutes, turning at halftime, until crisp and golden. Turn out onto wire racks to cool. Makes about 28 palmiers.

1 palmier: 93 Calories; 6.2 g Total Fat; 45 mg Sodium; 1 g Protein; 8 g Carbohydrate; trace Dietary Fibre

Pictured on page 36.

 Pie crust dough freezes better in a ball than if rolled out, and a ball takes up little room in the freezer. Cover the dough tightly in plastic wrap. Thaw at room temperature, in plastic wrap to prevent drying out, until only slightly chilled.

Upside-Down Treat

A light golden biscuit which, when inverted, is generously covered in warm pineapple, cherries and caramelized sugar. A classic comfort food.

Hard margarine (or butter)	2 tbsp.	30 mL
Brown sugar, packed	1/2 cup	125 mL
Can of crushed pineapple, drained	8 oz.	227 mL
Maraschino cherries, chopped	6	6
Tube of refrigerator country-style biscuits (10 biscuits per tube)	12 oz.	340 g

Coat 8 inch (20 cm) round pan with margarine. Sprinkle brown sugar over margarine. Scatter pineapple and cherries evenly over brown sugar.

Arrange biscuits close together over pineapple mixture. Bake in 425°F (220°C) oven for 15 minutes until lightly browned. Invert onto serving plate. Serve warm. Makes 10 biscuits.

1 biscuit: 163 Calories; 3.9 g Total Fat; 456 mg Sodium; 2 g Protein; 30 g Carbohydrate; trace Dietary Fibre

1. Amaretto Strawberries, page 69
2. Peanut Ice Cream Treat, page 82

Props Courtesy Of: Pfaltzgraff Canada

Cream-Layered Pastries

Layers of light puff pastry, strawberry jam and whipped cream.
Enjoy with a cup of coffee and imagine you are in a Parisian patisserie.

Package of frozen puff pastry (14 oz., 397 g, size), thawed according to package directions	1/2	1/2
Whipping cream	2/3 cup	150 mL
Strawberry jam, warmed	1/2 cup	125 mL

Icing (confectioner's) sugar, for dusting

Roll out pastry on lightly floured surface to about 9 x 9 inch (22 x 22 cm) square. Place on ungreased baking sheet. Bake in 400°F (205°C) oven for 10 to 12 minutes until golden and puffed. Let baking sheet stand on wire rack to cool. Split pastry in half horizontally into 2 layers. Cut each half into 6 rectangles.

Beat whipping cream in small bowl until soft peaks form. Spread 1 tbsp. (15 mL) jam on 1 side of 1 pastry rectangle. Spread 3 tbsp. (50 mL) whipped cream over jam. Top with another pastry rectangle. Spread 1 tbsp. (15 mL) jam over pastry rectangle. Spread 3 tbsp. (50 mL) whipped cream over jam. Top with another pastry rectangle. Repeat with remaining pastry rectangles, jam and whipped cream.

Dust with icing sugar. Makes 4 pastries.

1 pastry: 503 Calories; 32.5 g Total Fat; 156 mg Sodium; 5 g Protein; 51 g Carbohydrate; 1 g Dietary Fibre

Pictured on page 71.

1. Mango Macadamia Sandwich, page 76
2. Chocolate Raspberry Pie, page 80
3. Cran-Raspberry Ice, page 81

Sweet Orange Rolls

A delectable variation of sticky buns. These sweet and gooey rolls have a tantalizing orange flavour and a citrusy, sticky glaze. A favourite brunch item that will have your guests licking their fingers.

Biscuit mix	2 cups	500 mL
Orange (or vanilla) yogurt	1/2 cup	125 mL
Milk	1/4 cup	60 mL
All-purpose flour, approximately	1/4 cup	60 mL
Hard margarine (or butter)	2 tbsp.	30 mL
Brown sugar, packed	1/2 cup	125 mL
Finely grated orange peel	1 tsp.	5 mL
Ground cinnamon	1/8 – 1/4 tsp.	0.5 – 1 mL
ORANGE GLAZE		
Prepared orange juice	1 1/2 tbsp.	25 mL
Icing (confectioner's) sugar	2/3 cup	150 mL
Finely chopped walnuts (or pecans), optional	1 tbsp.	15 mL

Combine biscuit mix, yogurt and milk in medium bowl until just moistened. Turn out dough onto well-floured surface. Knead gently 10 to 12 times, sprinkling surface with more flour as needed to keep from sticking. Pat or roll out to 12 x 12 inch (30 x 30 cm) square.

Combine margarine, brown sugar, orange peel and cinnamon in small bowl. Spread evenly over dough. Roll up tightly, jelly roll-style. Pinch edge closed. Cut into 9 slices. Arrange, cut side down, in greased 9 x 9 inch (22 x 22 cm) pan. Bake in 375°F (190°C) oven for about 30 minutes until golden.

Orange Glaze: Stir orange juice into icing sugar in separate small bowl until smooth, adding enough icing sugar until barely pourable consistency. Drizzle over warm rolls.

Sprinkle with walnuts. Makes 9 rolls.

1 roll: 269 Calories; 7.6 g Total Fat; 430 mg Sodium; 4 g Protein; 47 g Carbohydrate; trace Dietary Fibre

Jam And Nut Tart

A golden pastry that combines the flavours of apricot, cinnamon, pecans and honey. A versatile dessert perfect for all seasons. Slice and eat like pizza.

Package of pie crust mix for 2 crust 9 inch (22 cm) pie	9 1/2 oz.	270 g
Granulated sugar	3 tbsp.	50 mL
Cold water	4 – 5 tbsp.	60 – 75 mL
Apricot (or peach) jam	1/2 cup	125 mL
Ground cinnamon	1/4 tsp.	1 mL
Finely chopped pecans	3/4 cup	175 mL
HONEY GLAZE		
Liquid honey, warmed	1 tbsp.	15 mL
Icing (confectioner's) sugar	2 1/2 tbsp.	37 mL
Warm water		

Combine pie crust mix and granulated sugar in medium bowl. Add cold water, 1 tbsp. (15 mL) at a time, stirring with fork until dough forms a ball. Divide into 2 portions. Form each portion into disc. Cover with plastic wrap. Chill for 30 minutes. Roll 1 disc out on lightly floured surface to 9 inch (22 cm) circle. Place on ungreased baking sheet.

Spread jam on pastry to within 3/4 inch (2 cm) of edge. Sprinkle with cinnamon and pecans. Dampen edge of pastry with water. Roll second disc out on lightly floured surface to 9 inch (22 cm) circle. Place over jam mixture. Press edges together with fork tines. Poke several steam holes in top of pastry. Bake, uncovered, in 375°F (190°C) oven for 20 to 30 minutes until golden.

Honey Glaze: Stir honey into icing sugar in small bowl until smooth. Stir in warm water, 1 drop at a time, until barely pourable consistency. Drizzle over warm tart. Cuts into 12 wedges.

1 wedge: 226 Calories; 12.4 g Total Fat; 175 mg Sodium; 2 g Protein; 28 g Carbohydrate; 1 g Dietary Fibre

A Touch Of Danish

Warm, soft biscuits stuffed with a cream cheese filling and decorated with a sweet, sticky glaze. These are best served warm with coffee or tea. Enjoy with jam for a fruity variation.

Tube of refrigerator country-style biscuits (10 biscuits per tube)	12 oz.	340 g
FILLING		
Cream cheese, softened	2 oz.	62 g
Granulated sugar	1 tbsp.	15 mL
Milk	2 tsp.	10 mL
GLAZE		
Icing (confectioner's) sugar	6 tbsp.	100 mL
Milk	2 tsp.	10 mL
Vanilla	1/8 tsp.	0.5 mL

Arrange biscuits about 1 1/2 inches (3.8 cm) apart on ungreased baking sheet. Make deep indentation in centre of each biscuit.

Filling: Mash cream cheese, granulated sugar and milk together well in small bowl. Makes about 1/4 cup (60 mL) filling. Spoon about 1 tsp. (5 mL) into each indentation. Bake in 425°F (220°C) oven for 10 to 12 minutes until lightly golden.

Glaze: Mix icing sugar, milk and vanilla in separate small bowl. Drizzle over warm biscuits. Serve immediately. Makes 10 biscuits.

1 biscuit: 131 Calories; 3.5 g Total Fat; 442 mg Sodium; 3 g Protein; 22 g Carbohydrate; 0 g Dietary Fibre

Pictured on page 36.

Paré Pointer
The plastic surgeon stood so close to the fire that he melted.

Pies & Pastries

Baklava

Pronounced BAHK-lah-vah. A classic dessert favourite of the Greek islands. Sweet, gooey syrup and walnut filling ooze out between layers of thin, flaky phyllo pastry. The only way to enjoy this sticky wonder is with your fingers.

Frozen phyllo pastry sheets, thawed according to package directions	12	12
Butter (not margarine), melted	1 cup	250 mL
Finely chopped walnuts (or pistachios)	2 cups	500 mL
SYRUP		
Granulated sugar	2 1/2 cups	625 mL
Water	1 1/2 cups	375 mL
Lemon juice	2 tbsp.	30 mL

Lay 1 pastry sheet on work surface. Keep remaining pastry sheets covered with damp tea towel to prevent drying out. Working quickly, brush pastry sheet with butter. Lay another pastry sheet over top. Brush with butter. Repeat with 4 more pastry sheets and butter. Cut pastry stack in half crosswise. Place 1/2 of stack in greased 9 x 13 inch (22 x 33 cm) dish. Top with remaining 1/2 of stack.

Sprinkle with walnuts. Repeat layering remaining pastry sheets and butter. Cut pastry in half crosswise. Place 1/2 of stack on top of walnuts. Top with remaining 1/2 of stack. Brush with butter. Make twelve 3 inch (7.5 cm) shallow square cuts into pastry sheets. Bake in 350°F (175°C) oven for about 50 minutes until golden. Cool.

Syrup: Combine sugar, water and lemon juice in medium saucepan. Heat and stir on medium until sugar is dissolved. Simmer, uncovered, without stirring, for about 15 minutes until slightly thickened. Makes 2 cups (500 mL) syrup. Pour hot syrup over cooled baklava. Cut each square into 2 triangles. Makes 24 triangles.

1 triangle: 252 Calories; 14.9 g Total Fat; 129 mg Sodium; 3 g Protein; 28 g Carbohydrate; 1 g Dietary Fibre

Pumpkin Tartlets

Warmly spiced pumpkin pie tartlets with a rich, creamy texture.
A heavenly aroma will fill your house while these treats are in the oven.

PASTRY

All-purpose flour	2 cups	500 mL
Brown sugar, packed	1 tbsp.	15 mL
Salt	1/2 tsp.	2 mL
Hard margarine (or butter), chilled, cut up	1 cup	250 mL
Water	1/3 cup	75 mL

FILLING

Can of pure pumpkin (without spices)	14 oz.	398 mL
Can of sweetened condensed milk	11 oz.	300 mL
All-purpose flour	2 tbsp.	30 mL
Large eggs	2	2
Ground cinnamon	3/4 tsp.	4 mL
Ground ginger	1/2 tsp.	2 mL
Ground nutmeg	1/4 tsp.	1 mL
Ground allspice	1/4 tsp.	1 mL
Salt	1/4 tsp.	1 mL

Whipped cream (or frozen whipped topping, thawed), for garnish

Pastry: Combine flour, brown sugar and salt in large bowl. Cut in margarine until consistency of coarse crumbs.

Drizzle water over top. Stir with fork until dough forms a ball. Roll out on lightly floured surface to 1/8 inch (3 mm) thickness. Cut into 2 1/2 inch (6.4 cm) rounds. Line tartlet pans or mini-muffin cups.

Filling: Stir pumpkin and condensed milk in medium bowl. Sprinkle with flour. Mix well.

Add next 6 ingredients. Stir until smooth. Makes 3 1/4 cups (800 mL) filling. Spoon 1 1/2 tbsp. (25 mL) filling into each pastry shell. Bake in 375°F (190°C) oven for about 20 minutes until wooden pick inserted in centre of tartlet comes out clean.

(continued on next page)

Pies & Pastries

Garnish with whipped cream. Makes 36 tartlets.

1 tartlet: 121 Calories; 6.7 g Total Fat; 130 mg Sodium; 2 g Protein; 13 g Carbohydrate; trace Dietary Fibre

PUMPKIN PIE: Line 9 inch (22 cm) pie plate with 1/2 of pastry. Freeze remaining pastry to use another time. Add filling. Bake in 425°F (220°C) oven for 10 minutes. Reduce heat to 325°F (160°C). Bake for about 1 hour until knife inserted near centre comes out clean. Cool. Garnish with whipped cream. Cuts into 8 wedges.

Lemon Pastries

Golden, flaky puff pastry with a sweet creamy filling and a sharp lemony tang.

Package of frozen puff pastry, thawed according to package directions	14 oz.	397 g
LEMON FILLING		
Finely grated lemon zest	2 tsp.	10 mL
Freshly squeezed lemon juice	1/4 cup	60 mL
Granulated sugar	1/2 cup	125 mL
Whipping cream	1/2 cup	125 mL
Large eggs	2	2

Icing (confectioner's) sugar, for dusting

Roll pastry halves out to 1/8 inch (3 mm) thickness. Cut six 4 inch (10 cm) rounds from each pastry half. Press rounds into lightly greased muffin cups. Put scrunched up foil ball, about 1 1/4 inches (3 cm) in diameter, into each cup to fill. Bake in 400°F (205°C) oven for 10 to 15 minutes until lightly golden. Let stand in pan with foil balls in place until cool. Remove foil.

Lemon Filling: Whisk first 5 ingredients in 4 cup (1 L) liquid measure until well combined. Let stand for 5 minutes. Stir. Fill pastry cups 3/4 full. Bake in 325°F (160°C) oven for 20 to 25 minutes until almost set in centre. Let stand in pan for 30 minutes before removing to wire rack to cool. Chill.

Dust with icing sugar just before serving. Makes 12 pastries.

1 pastry: 262 Calories; 16.8 g Total Fat; 97 mg Sodium; 4 g Protein; 25 g Carbohydrate; trace Dietary Fibre

Creamy Banana Pie

Banana cream pie made easy! This pie is light and fluffy with a nice creamy texture. A delicious finale to any meal.

Brown sugar, packed	1/3 cup	75 mL
Cornstarch	3 tbsp.	50 mL
All-purpose flour	2 tbsp.	30 mL
Salt	1/4 tsp.	1 mL
Milk	2 cups	500 mL
Large eggs	2	2
Half-and-half cream	1/3 cup	75 mL
Hard margarine (or butter)	2 tsp.	10 mL
Vanilla	1 1/2 tsp.	7 mL
Medium bananas, diced	2	2
Baked 9 inch (22 cm) pie shell (or graham cracker crust)	1	1
Envelope of dessert topping (not prepared)	1	1
Milk	1/2 cup	125 mL
Vanilla	1/2 tsp.	2 mL

Sliced banana, for garnish

Combine brown sugar, cornstarch, flour and salt in medium saucepan. Stir in first amount of milk. Heat and stir on medium for about 6 minutes until boiling and thickened. Remove from heat.

Beat eggs and cream with fork in small bowl. Whisk into hot milk mixture. Heat and stir for about 3 minutes until beginning to boil. Remove from heat.

Stir in margarine, first amount of vanilla and diced banana.

Turn out into pie shell. Cover with plastic wrap directly on surface to prevent skin from forming. Chill for at least 2 hours until set.

Beat dessert topping and second amounts of milk and vanilla until stiff peaks form. Spread over filling.

Garnish with sliced banana just before serving. Cuts into 8 wedges.

1 wedge: 270 Calories; 11.6 g Total Fat; 259 mg Sodium; 6 g Protein; 36 g Carbohydrate; 1 g Dietary Fibre

Pies & Pastries

Lemon Lime Pie

Indulgently sweet, yet tart enough to give your cheeks a little pucker.
This pie has a tantalizing lime green hue. It begs to be tasted.

Can of sweetened condensed milk	11 oz.	300 mL
Egg yolks (large)	4	4
Lime juice	1/4 cup	60 mL
Lemon juice	1/4 cup	60 mL
Egg white (large), room temperature	1	1
Drop of green food colouring (optional)	1	1
Finely grated lemon zest	1/2 tbsp.	7 mL
Baked 9 inch (22 cm) pie shell	1	1
Egg whites (large), room temperature	3	3
Cream of tartar	1/2 tsp.	2 mL
Granulated sugar	1/3 cup	75 mL

Combine condensed milk, egg yolks, lime juice and lemon juice in medium bowl. Mix well.

Beat first egg white in separate medium bowl until stiff peaks form. Fold into condensed milk mixture along with food colouring and lemon zest.

Pour into pie shell. Set aside.

Beat second amount of egg whites and cream of tartar in separate medium bowl until soft peaks form. Add sugar, 1 tbsp. (15 mL) at a time, until stiff peaks form and sugar is dissolved. Spoon over filling, sealing edges to crust. Bake in 350°F (175°C) oven for about 14 minutes until browned. Let stand on wire rack to cool to room temperature. Chill for at least 8 hours or overnight. Cuts into 8 wedges.

1 wedge: 313 Calories; 11.9 g Total Fat; 195 mg Sodium; 8 g Protein; 45 g Carbohydrate; trace Dietary Fibre

KEY LIME PIE: Omit lime juice and lemon juice. Use 1/2 cup (125 mL) key lime juice.

Rich Chocolate Pudding

This rich chocolate pudding is baked right in the pan.
A dusting of icing sugar gives a look of elegance. Serve in parfait glasses
with a cup of coffee or an after-dinner liqueur.

All-purpose flour	1 cup	250 mL
Baking powder	2 tsp.	10 mL
Cocoa, sifted if lumpy	3 tbsp.	50 mL
Salt	1/2 tsp.	2 mL
Granulated sugar	1 cup	250 mL
Milk	1/2 cup	125 mL
Hard margarine (or butter), melted	2 tbsp.	30 mL
Vanilla	1 tsp.	5 mL
Brown sugar, packed	3/4 cup	175 mL
Cocoa, sifted if lumpy	1/3 cup	75 mL
Hot water	1 3/4 cups	425 mL

Icing (confectioner's) sugar, for dusting

Stir first 5 ingredients in large bowl.

Add milk, margarine and vanilla. Stir until smooth. Pour into greased 2 quart (2 L) shallow dish.

Stir brown sugar and second amount of cocoa in small bowl. Sprinkle evenly over pudding mixture.

Carefully pour hot water over top. Bake in 350°F (175°C) oven for 50 to 55 minutes until pudding is set.

Dust with icing sugar just before serving. Serves 8.

1 serving: 292 Calories; 4 g Total Fat; 293 mg Sodium; 3 g Protein; 65 g Carbohydrate; 2 g Dietary Fibre

Sticky Date Pudding

A sticky, cake-like pudding with a delicious buttery caramel sauce.
Based on the ever-popular English sticky toffee pudding. Serve warm.

Water	1 1/3 cups	325 mL
Seeded dates, coarsely chopped	1 1/3 cups	325 mL
Baking soda	1 tsp.	5 mL
Hard margarine (or butter), softened	1/3 cup	75 mL
Brown sugar, packed	3/4 cup	175 mL
Large eggs	2	2
All-purpose flour	1 cup	250 mL
Baking powder	2 tsp.	10 mL
Ground cinnamon	1 tsp.	5 mL
WARM CARAMEL SAUCE		
Whipping cream	1/2 cup	125 mL
Hard margarine (or butter)	1/2 cup	125 mL
Brown sugar, packed	1/2 cup	125 mL

Bring water to a boil in medium saucepan. Add dates. Stir. Remove from heat. Add baking soda. Stir. Let stand for 10 minutes. Stir. Pour into large bowl.

Add next 6 ingredients. Beat until well combined. Pour into greased and parchment paper-lined 8 inch (20 cm) springform pan. Bake in 350°F (175°C) oven for 50 to 55 minutes until wooden pick inserted in centre comes out clean. Let stand in pan for 10 minutes before turning out onto wire rack to cool. Cuts into 8 wedges.

Warm Caramel Sauce: Combine whipping cream, margarine and brown sugar in large saucepan. Heat and stir on medium for 3 to 5 minutes until margarine is melted. Bring to a boil. Boil, without stirring, for about 5 minutes until slightly thickened. Makes 1 cup (250 mL) sauce. Serve with pudding. Serves 8.

1 serving: 530 Calories; 26.8 g Total Fat; 508 mg Sodium; 4 g Protein; 72 g Carbohydrate; 3 g Dietary Fibre

Pictured on page 108 and on back cover.

Coconut Crunch Pudding

Rich, creamy coconut pudding layered with a cookie-type crumble.
Serve in individual parfait glasses with a dollop of whipped cream.

COCONUT CRUNCH

All-purpose flour	1/2 cup	125 mL
Brown sugar, packed	2 tbsp.	30 mL
Hard margarine (or butter), chilled	1/4 cup	60 mL
Flake coconut	1/2 cup	125 mL

COCONUT CUSTARD

Homogenized milk	1 1/3 cups	325 mL
All-purpose flour	2 tbsp.	30 mL
Cornstarch	2 tbsp.	30 mL
Granulated sugar	1/3 cup	75 mL
Salt	1/4 tsp.	1 mL
Half-and-half cream	2/3 cup	150 mL
Egg yolks (large), fork-beaten	2	2
Hard margarine (or butter)	2 tsp.	10 mL
Flake coconut	1/2 cup	125 mL
Coconut flavouring	2 tsp.	10 mL
Whipped cream (or dessert topping, prepared), optional	1 cup	250 mL

Coconut Crunch: Combine flour and brown sugar in medium bowl. Cut in margarine until crumbly.

Add coconut. Rub mixture between palms of hands until no lumps of margarine remain. Turn into ungreased 9 x 9 inch (22 x 22 cm) pan. Bake in 400°F (205°C) oven for about 20 minutes, stirring with fork every 5 minutes, until golden. Stir to break up large clumps. Cool. Makes 3 1/3 cups (825 mL) crunch.

Coconut Custard: Heat milk, uncovered, in medium saucepan on medium for about 5 minutes, stirring occasionally, until bubbles begin to form around side of pan. Do not boil.

Combine flour, cornstarch, sugar and salt in small bowl. Gradually stir in half-and-half cream until smooth. Slowly stir into milk. Heat and stir for about 2 minutes until boiling and thickened. Remove from heat.

(continued on next page)

Combine 1/4 cup (60 mL) milk mixture and egg yolks in small dish. Mix well. Stir into milk mixture. Heat and stir on medium for about 2 minutes until thickened. Remove from heat.

Stir in margarine, coconut and flavouring. Cover with plastic wrap directly on surface to prevent skin from forming. Makes 2 1/3 cups (575 mL) custard.

Layer crunch and custard, repeating layers several times, in clear serving bowl or in 4 individual parfait glasses, reserving 1/3 cup (75 mL) crunch. Top with whipped cream. Sprinkle reserved crunch over whipped cream. Serves 4.

1 serving: 535 Calories; 30.4 g Total Fat; 410 mg Sodium; 8 g Protein; 59 g Carbohydrate; 2 g Dietary Fibre

Pictured on page 125.

Cinnamon Bread Pudding

A unique variation of cinnamon bread. The sweet chunks of apples give this pudding a fruity tartness and the pecans add a satisfying crunch.

Large un-iced cinnamon buns, cut into 1 inch (2.5 cm) pieces (about 3 cups, 750 mL)	2	2
Dried apples, chopped	1/3 cup	75 mL
Milk	2 2/3 cups	650 mL
Large eggs	3	3
Brown sugar, packed	1/4 cup	60 mL
Pecans, chopped	1/3 cup	75 mL

Scatter cinnamon bun pieces and apples in greased 2 quart (2 L) shallow dish.

Whisk milk, eggs and brown sugar together in medium bowl or 4 cup (1 L) liquid measure until well combined. Carefully pour over cinnamon bun pieces.

Sprinkle with pecans. Let stand for 10 minutes. Bake, uncovered, in 350°F (175°C) oven for about 50 minutes until set and knife inserted in centre comes out clean. Let stand in pan for 15 minutes before serving. Serves 6.

1 serving: 292 Calories; 13.3 g Total Fat; 212 mg Sodium; 9 g Protein; 35 g Carbohydrate; 1 g Dietary Fibre

Old-Fashioned Apple Cobbler

Cinnamon-spiced apples with a golden brown biscuit topping.
A good old-fashioned comfort food. Serve hot with
a dollop of ice cream or whipped cream.

APPLE FILLING

Medium cooking apples (such as McIntosh), peeled, cored, sliced	6	6
Granulated sugar	1/2 cup	125 mL
Ground cinnamon	1/2 tsp.	2 mL
Water	3/4 cup	175 mL

TOPPING

All-purpose flour	1 cup	250 mL
Granulated sugar	1/4 cup	60 mL
Baking powder	2 tsp.	10 mL
Salt	1/2 tsp.	2 mL
Hard margarine (or butter), chilled	3 tbsp.	50 mL
Cold milk	1/2 cup	125 mL

Apple Filling: Put first 4 ingredients into large saucepan. Bring to a boil on medium-high. Reduce heat. Simmer, uncovered, for 5 to 7 minutes on medium until apple is tender. Turn into greased 1 1/2 quart (1.5 L) casserole. Keep warm in 400°F (205°C) oven while preparing topping.

Topping: Measure flour, sugar, baking powder and salt into medium bowl. Cut in margarine until crumbly.

Add milk. Mix until just moistened. Drop by spoonfuls over hot apple mixture. Bake, uncovered, for 20 to 25 minutes until wooden pick inserted in centre comes out clean. Serves 6 to 8.

1 serving: 318 Calories; 6.6 g Total Fat; 401 mg Sodium; 3 g Protein; 64 g Carbohydrate; 3 g Dietary Fibre

Peach Crumble

Tangy sweet peaches with a delicious rolled oat and brown sugar topping.
As it bakes, the peachy syrup bubbles deliciously through the golden oat topping.
Serve hot with ice cream or half-and-half cream.

Frozen sliced peaches, thawed	4 cups	1 L
Brown sugar, packed	1/4 cup	60 mL
Granulated sugar	1/4 cup	60 mL
Minute tapioca	1 tbsp.	15 mL
Ground cinnamon, sprinkle		
Quick-cooking rolled oats (not instant)	6 tbsp.	100 mL
All-purpose flour	1/4 cup	60 mL
Brown sugar, packed	1/4 cup	60 mL
Salt	1/8 tsp.	0.5 mL
Hard margarine (or butter)	3 tbsp.	50 mL

Turn peaches into greased 1 1/2 quart (1.5 L) shallow casserole.

Combine first amount of brown sugar, granulated sugar, tapioca and cinnamon in small bowl. Sprinkle over peaches.

Mix rolled oats, flour, second amount of brown sugar and salt in medium bowl. Cut in margarine until crumbly. Sprinkle over peaches. Pack down slightly with palm of hand. Bake, uncovered, in 350°F (175°C) oven for 50 to 55 minutes until golden and centre is bubbly. Serves 6.

1 serving: 292 Calories; 6.4 g Total Fat; 133 mg Sodium; 2 g Protein; 59 g Carbohydrate; 2 g Dietary Fibre

Mango Raspberry Trifles

A fun variation of the traditional trifle. Mango and fresh raspberries make this a very colourful dessert. Assemble in individual wine glasses and serve after a special meal.

Orange-flavoured liqueur (such as Grand Marnier)	2 tbsp.	30 mL
Prepared orange juice	1/4 cup	60 mL
Mascarpone cheese	1 1/3 cups	325 mL
Icing (confectioner's) sugar	1/3 cup	75 mL
Ladyfingers	8	8
Cans of sliced mango, with syrup (14 oz., 398 mL, each), drained, sliced diagonally	2	2
Fresh raspberries	1 1/3 cups	325 mL

Combine liqueur and orange juice in small bowl.

Mash or beat cheese and icing sugar in separate small bowl.

Break each ladyfinger in half. Dip each into orange juice mixture. Place 2 halves in bottom of each of 4 serving glasses. Divide 1/2 of mango over ladyfingers. Spoon or pipe 1/2 of cheese mixture over mango. Divide 1/2 of raspberries and sprinkle over cheese mixture. Repeat layers. Chill for 1 to 3 hours. Serves 4.

1 serving: 553 Calories; 31.3 g Total Fat; 277 mg Sodium; 10 g Protein; 58 g Carbohydrate; 6 g Dietary Fibre

Pictured on page 108 and on back cover.

1. Espresso Sundae, page 79
2. White Chocolate Sauce, page 111
3. Cola Zucchini Cake, page 22
4. Coffee Meringues, page 56

Props Courtesy Of: Canhome Global

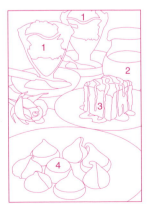

Chantilly Crumbs

This sweet, chewy, nutty dessert is so easy to prepare. Top with a dollop of whipped cream and garnish with nuts, cherries or shaved chocolate. Or all three!

Brown sugar, packed	1 cup	250 mL
All-purpose flour	1/3 cup	75 mL
Large egg, fork-beaten	1	1
Finely chopped mixed nuts	1/2 cup	125 mL
Baking soda	1/2 tsp.	2 mL
Whipping cream	1 cup	250 mL
Granulated sugar	1 tbsp.	15 mL
Vanilla	1/2 tsp.	2 mL

Measure first 5 ingredients into ungreased 8 × 8 inch (20 × 20 cm) pan. Stir until evenly mixed. Bake in 325°F (160°C) oven for 25 minutes. Cool. Turn into larger container. Break into small crumbly pieces.

Beat whipping cream, granulated sugar and vanilla in medium bowl until stiff peaks form. Fold crumb mixture into whipped cream mixture. Chill for 2 hours. To serve, divide and spoon into 6 sherbet dishes or champagne glasses. Serves 6.

1 serving: 388 Calories; 20.6 g Total Fat; 148 mg Sodium; 5 g Protein; 48 g Carbohydrate; 1 g Dietary Fibre

1. Mango Raspberry Trifles, page 106
2. Lemon Poppy Loaf, page 24
3. Sticky Date Pudding, page 101
4. Pastry Triangles With Pears, page 86

Props Courtesy Of: Cornell Trading Ltd.
La Cache

Coffee Custard Sauce

A creamy, coffee-flavoured sauce with a warming hint of brandy.
Delicious over ice cream or served with a rich chocolate cake.

Whipping cream	1 cup	250 mL
Instant coffee granules	1 tbsp.	15 mL
Egg yolks (large)	2	2
Granulated sugar	1/4 cup	60 mL
Brandy (or 1/4 tsp., 1 mL, brandy flavouring)	1 tbsp.	15 mL

Heat whipping cream, uncovered, in heavy medium saucepan on medium-high for about 5 minutes until bubbles begin to form around edge of saucepan. Remove from heat.

Add coffee granules. Stir until coffee is dissolved.

Beat egg yolks and sugar together in small bowl until light and fluffy. Add 1/4 of hot whipping cream mixture to egg yolk mixture. Mix well. Stir into whipping cream mixture. Heat and stir on low for about 10 minutes until thickened and mixture coats back of spoon. Remove from heat.

Add brandy. Stir. Makes about 1 2/3 cups (400 mL).

2 tbsp. (30 mL): 81 Calories; 6.6 g Total Fat; 8 mg Sodium; 1 g Protein; 5 g Carbohydrate; 0 g Dietary Fibre

Paré Pointer

Before spaghetti could be sold commercially,
it had to pasta taste test.

White Chocolate Sauce

The rich, sweet, creamy taste of white chocolate with a tempting
hint of brandy. A white chocolate lover's dream come true!
Excellent with Cola Zucchini Cake, page 22.

Granulated sugar	1/4 cup	60 mL
Whipping cream	1 cup	250 mL
Vanilla	1 tsp.	5 mL
Brandy (or 1/2 tsp., 2 mL, brandy flavouring)	2 tbsp.	30 mL
White chocolate baking squares (1 oz., 28 g, each), chopped	6	6

Combine sugar and whipping cream in heavy medium saucepan. Heat and stir on medium for 1 to 2 minutes until sugar is dissolved. Boil gently for 3 minutes.

Add vanilla and brandy. Stir. Remove from heat.

Stir in chocolate until melted and sauce is smooth. Cool. Makes about 1 2/3 cups (400 mL).

2 tbsp. (30 mL): 140 Calories; 9.5 g Total Fat; 17 mg Sodium; 1 g Protein; 12 g Carbohydrate; 0 g Dietary Fibre

Pictured on page 107.

 The grayish-white film on chocolate is called bloom and is the result of cocoa butter or sugar crystals rising to the surface after exposure to varying temperatures. It does not affect flavour and after chocolate is melted, it will disappear.

Maple Walnut Sauce

A delightfully rich and smooth caramel sauce with maple flavouring and crunchy walnuts. This sweet, gooey sauce is magical on ice cream or Christmas pudding.

Brown sugar, packed	1 cup	250 mL
All-purpose flour	3 tbsp.	50 mL
Water	1 1/2 cups	375 mL
Corn syrup	2 tbsp.	30 mL
Hard margarine (or butter)	2 tbsp.	30 mL
Maple flavouring	1 tsp.	5 mL
Chopped walnuts	1 cup	250 mL

Combine brown sugar and flour in 4 cup (1 L) liquid measure. Stir well.

Stir in water. Add remaining 4 ingredients. Stir. Microwave, uncovered, on high (100%) for about 5 minutes, stirring after each minute, until boiling and thickened. Makes 2 1/2 cups (625 mL).

2 tbsp. (30 mL): 101 Calories; 4.7 g Total Fat; 19 mg Sodium; 2 g Protein; 14 g Carbohydrate; trace Dietary Fibre

tip *To quickly chop nuts, place in a resealable plastic bag and roll a rolling pin over top until desired consistency.*

Chocolate Fudge Sauce

This velvety smooth chocolate fudge sauce is rich and oh-so-decadent.
Enjoy it over cake, ice cream, crêpes, fresh fruit or anything that
needs a rich chocolate lift.

Semi-sweet chocolate chips	1 cup	250 mL
Hard margarine (or butter)	1/4 cup	60 mL
Corn syrup	2/3 cup	150 mL
Hot water	2/3 cup	150 mL
Instant coffee granules	1 1/2 tsp.	7 mL
Salt	1/16 tsp.	0.5 mL
Icing (confectioner's) sugar	1 cup	250 mL
Vanilla	1 1/2 tsp.	7 mL

Measure first 6 ingredients into medium saucepan. Heat on medium for about 10 minutes, stirring frequently, until margarine is melted and mixture is smooth. Remove from heat.

Gradually beat in icing sugar, 1/4 cup (60 mL) at a time, until consistency of medium-thick sauce. Beat in vanilla. Makes 2 1/3 cups (575 mL).

2 tbsp. (30 mL): 129 Calories; 5.3 g Total Fat; 47 mg Sodium; trace Protein; 22 g Carbohydrate; 1 g Dietary Fibre

Paré Pointer
Everyone knows a pediatrician is a doctor with very little patients.

Quick Caramel Fondue

Hot melted caramel with a tantalizing rum flavour! So creamy and rich.
Try as a dip for fresh fruit pieces or cubes of white snack cake.
And, of course, this is perfect over ice cream.

Caramels (about 11 oz., 310 g)	40	40
Milk	1/3 cup	75 mL
Rum flavouring	1 tsp.	5 mL

Heat and stir caramels, milk and flavouring in medium saucepan on medium-low for about 10 minutes until smooth. Carefully pour into fondue pot to no more than 2/3 full. Place over low heat. Makes about 1 cup (250 mL).

2 tbsp. (30 mL): 146 Calories; 3.1 g Total Fat; 96 mg Sodium; 2 g Protein; 29 g Carbohydrate; trace Dietary Fibre

Suggested Dippers: Apple and banana slices; Chocolate Snack Cake pieces, page 22; White Snack Cake pieces, page 23; cookie pieces; marshmallows. Serve with dish of chopped nuts to roll dipped food in.

 Choose firm fruit and cakes for dipping in dessert fondues. Delicate fruit, such as watermelon or raspberries, and crumbly cakes or doughnuts may not stay on fondue forks and may get lost in the fondue pot.

Orange Butter

This buttery orange spread is at home on the weekend brunch table.
Delicious on muffins, rolls, fresh bread, pancakes and crêpes.

Butter (or hard margarine), softened	1/2 cup	125 mL
Icing (confectioner's) sugar	6 tbsp.	100 mL
Orange marmalade	1/4 cup	60 mL

Beat butter, icing sugar and marmalade together in small bowl. Pack into small mold or airtight container. Makes 2/3 cup (150 mL).

2 tsp. (10 mL): 75 Calories; 5.8 g Total Fat; 62 mg Sodium; trace Protein; 6 g Carbohydrate; 0 g Dietary Fibre

Strawberry Spread

A fresh, fruity spread with the warm summery taste of strawberries.
Delicious on bagels or muffins.

Mashed fresh (or frozen whole, thawed to room temperature and drained) strawberries	2/3 cup	150 mL
Granulated sugar	2 tbsp.	30 mL
Icing (confectioner's) sugar	1/4 cup	60 mL
Hard margarine (or butter), softened	1/2 cup	125 mL

Beat all 4 ingredients together in small bowl for about 10 minutes until smooth. Pack into mold or shape into small balls. Cover. Chill. Makes 1 1/4 cups (300 mL).

1 tbsp. (15 mL): 54 Calories; 4.7 g Total Fat; 54 mg Sodium; trace Protein; 3 g Carbohydrate; trace Dietary Fibre

Pictured on page 144.

Peach Cream Cheese Spread

Cream cheese spread with the subtle fragrance and sweetness of peaches and the refreshing zing of ginger. Great spread on a toasted bagel or English muffin.

Block of cream cheese, softened	4 oz.	125 g
Brown sugar, packed	2 tbsp.	30 mL
Finely chopped (fresh or canned) peaches	1/4 cup	60 mL
Finely minced crystallized ginger	1 – 2 tbsp.	15 – 30 mL

Beat cream cheese and brown sugar together in medium bowl until smooth.

Add peaches and ginger. Beat until well combined. Cover. Chill for at least 1 hour to allow flavours to blend. Makes 1 cup (250 mL).

1 tbsp. (15 mL): 34 Calories; 2.6 g Total Fat; 23 mg Sodium; 1 g Protein; 2 g Carbohydrate; trace Dietary Fibre

Raspberry Spread

A rich, creamy spread with juicy sweet raspberries throughout. A very easy-to-prepare spread to dress up your toasted bagel, English muffin or toast.

Block of cream cheese, softened	4 oz.	125 g
Icing (confectioner's) sugar	1/3 cup	75 mL
Frozen (or fresh) raspberries, thawed and drained	1/3 cup	75 mL
Finely grated lemon zest	1/4 tsp.	1 mL

Beat cream cheese and icing sugar in medium bowl until smooth and light.

Add raspberries and lemon zest. Beat until well combined. Cover. Chill for at least 1 hour to allow flavours to blend. Makes 3/4 cup (175 mL).

1 tbsp. (15 mL): 55 Calories; 3.4 g Total Fat; 29 mg Sodium; 1 g Protein; 5 g Carbohydrate; trace Dietary Fibre

Pictured on page 144.

Ginger Cheese Spread

Creamy and smooth with zingy gingersnap crumbs throughout.
A melt-in-your-mouth spread that is unique and easy to prepare.
Delicious on bagels, English muffins or toast.

Block of cream cheese, softened	4 oz.	125 g
Hard margarine (or butter)	1/4 cup	60 mL
Gingersnaps, processed into fine crumbs (about 8)	1/3 cup	75 mL
Icing (confectioner's) sugar	1/3 cup	75 mL

Beat cream cheese and margarine until smooth and fluffy.

Add gingersnap crumbs and icing sugar. Beat until smooth. Cover. Chill for at least 1 hour to allow flavours to blend. Makes about 1 cup (250 mL).

1 tbsp. (15 mL): 76 Calories; 5.9 g Total Fat; 74 mg Sodium; 1 g Protein; 5 g Carbohydrate; trace Dietary Fibre

Pictured on page 144.

 Too much heat cooks chocolate and makes it firm. Use lowest heat to melt, stirring often until melted. Do not overheat.

Yogurt Fruit Dip

This dip works well with any flavour of yogurt. It is mild, creamy and fresh tasting. Use as a fruit dip or spoon over your favourite dessert. So quick and easy to prepare.

Strawberry yogurt (stir before measuring)	1/2 cup	125 mL
Icing (confectioner's) sugar	1 tbsp.	15 mL
Frozen whipped topping, thawed	1/2 cup	125 mL

Fold yogurt and icing sugar into whipped topping in small bowl. Makes 3/4 cup (175 mL).

2 tbsp. (30 mL): 46 Calories; 1.9 g Total Fat; 12 mg Sodium; 1 g Protein; 6 g Carbohydrate; 0 g Dietary Fibre

Pictured on page 144.

Hot Mocha Dip

Another sweet treat to delight the chocolate and coffee lovers. This dip is very rich, very flavourful and very decadent. Your guests would never believe how easy it is to prepare, so why tell them? Perfect for dunking fresh fruit and cookies or spooning over ice cream.

Semi-sweet chocolate chips	2 cups	500 mL
Whipping cream	1/3 cup	75 mL
Prepared very strong coffee (or 2 tbsp., 30 mL, coffee-flavoured liqueur, such as Kahlúa)	1/3 cup	75 mL
Vanilla	1/2 tsp.	2 mL

Combine all 4 ingredients in medium saucepan. Heat and stir on medium-low until smooth. Makes 1 1/2 cups (375 mL).

2 tbsp. (30 mL): 157 Calories; 10.7 g Total Fat; 6 mg Sodium; 1 g Protein; 18 g Carbohydrate; 2 g Dietary Fibre

Marshmallow Pudding Dip

*A big hit with kids and easy enough for them to help you prepare.
This sweet, sticky, creamy dip can be made with any pudding flavour.
Perfect for dipping bananas or other fresh fruit.*

Jar of marshmallow creme	7 oz.	198 g
Milk	2 1/2 cups	625 mL
Instant pudding powder (4 serving size), your choice	1	1
Vanilla	1 tsp.	5 mL

Beat marshmallow creme in large bowl, slowly adding milk until well combined.

Add pudding powder and vanilla. Beat on low for about 2 minutes until smooth. Let stand for 5 minutes to thicken slightly. Makes 3 1/2 cups (875 mL).

2 tbsp. (30 mL): 44 Calories; 0.3 g Total Fat; 65 mg Sodium; 1 g Protein; 10 g Carbohydrate; 0 g Dietary Fibre

 To prevent commercial marshmallows from drying out, store in the freezer. Thawed or fresh, marshmallows are easily cut with scissors when ready to use.

Peanut Munch

A variation of the crisp rice square classic. Peanuts add an enjoyable crunch to this sticky, chewy snack. Label for the kids' lunch boxes or afternoon snack.

Rice squares cereal	1 cup	250 mL
Crisp rice cereal	1 cup	250 mL
Unsalted peanuts	2/3 cup	150 mL
Hard margarine (or butter)	2 tbsp.	30 mL
White corn syrup	1/4 cup	60 mL
Smooth peanut butter	1/4 cup	60 mL
Vanilla	1/2 tsp.	2 mL
Granulated sugar	4 tsp.	20 mL

Combine both cereals and peanuts in large bowl.

Heat margarine, corn syrup and peanut butter in small saucepan on low until smooth and bubbly. Remove from heat.

Stir in vanilla. Pour over cereal mixture. Stir until well coated. Spread out on large greased baking sheet with sides.

Sprinkle with 2 tsp. (10 mL) sugar. Bake in 350°F (175°C) oven for 5 minutes. Stir. Sprinkle with remaining sugar. Bake for 5 minutes. Let baking sheet stand on wire rack, stirring once or twice, to cool. Makes 3 cups (750 mL).

1/3 cup (75 mL): 202 Calories; 12.2 g Total Fat; 144 mg Sodium; 5 g Protein; 20 g Carbohydrate; 2 g Dietary Fibre

Paré Pointer

A clever carpenter always nails down his agreements.

Crunchy Cereal Toss

A toss of cereal, nuts, seeds and dried fruit with an apricot candy coating.
These delicious, crunchy, chewy pieces are perfect for snacking.

Hard margarine (or butter)	1/3 cup	75 mL
Granulated sugar	1/3 cup	75 mL
Apricot (or mango) jam, large pieces finely chopped	1/2 cup	125 mL
Rice squares cereal	3 cups	750 mL
Slivered almonds	1/3 cup	75 mL
Pecan halves	1/3 cup	75 mL
Dried apricots (or golden raisins), diced	1/2 cup	125 mL
Sunflower seeds	2 tbsp.	30 mL

Heat and stir margarine, sugar and jam in small saucepan on medium until sugar and jam are dissolved.

Combine remaining 5 ingredients in large bowl. Pour margarine mixture over top. Toss until well coated. Spread out on ungreased baking sheet. Bake in 325°F (160°C) oven for 25 minutes. Let baking sheet stand on wire rack to cool. Tap baking sheet on counter to loosen cereal mixture. Break into bite-size pieces. Makes 3 1/2 cups (875 mL).

1/3 cup (75 mL): 237 Calories; 11.7 g Total Fat; 177 mg Sodium; 3 g Protein; 33 g Carbohydrate; 1 g Dietary Fibre

tip   *To achieve even baking, be sure the baking sheets, cake pan or muffin pans do not touch the sides of the oven. This prevents the air from circulating properly.*

Peanut Butter Popcorn

A peanutty variation of caramel corn. This crunchy, sticky treat is the perfect companion to curl up with on movie night.

Unpopped corn	1/2 cup	125 mL
Golden corn syrup	3/4 cup	175 mL
Brown sugar, packed	1/2 cup	125 mL
Smooth peanut butter	3/4 cup	175 mL
Vanilla	1 tsp.	5 mL
Roasted salted peanuts	2 cups	500 mL

Pop corn, in hot air popper, into very large bowl or container.

Stir corn syrup and brown sugar together in medium saucepan on medium for 4 to 5 minutes until boiling and sugar is dissolved. Remove from heat.

Stir in peanut butter and vanilla until smooth. Stir in peanuts. Gradually pour over popped corn, while stirring, until coated. Spread out on large greased baking sheets or on waxed paper-covered surface. Let stand, uncovered, stirring once or twice, until cool. Makes 18 cups (4.5 L).

1/2 cup (125 mL): 131 Calories; 7.3 g Total Fat; 108 mg Sodium; 4 g Protein; 15 g Carbohydrate; 2 g Dietary Fibre

White Chocolate Popcorn

The ultimate snack for those who love white chocolate and caramel corn—the perfect "pick-me-up" snack.

White chocolate candy bars (3 1/2 oz., 100 g, each), chopped	3	3
Bag of caramel-coated popcorn and peanuts (about 5 cups, 1.25 L)	7 oz.	200 g
Slivered almonds, toasted (see Tip, page 79)	1/2 cup	125 mL

(continued on next page)

Snacks & Treats

Heat chocolate in medium saucepan on lowest heat, stirring often, until almost melted. Do not overheat. Remove from heat. Stir until smooth.

Spread popcorn on foil-lined baking sheet. Drizzle chocolate evenly over popcorn. Stir. Sprinkle with almonds. Chill until set. Break into bite-size pieces. Makes about 5 1/2 cups (1.4 L).

1/2 cup (125 mL): 255 Calories; 13 g Total Fat; 79 mg Sodium; 4 g Protein; 33 g Carbohydrate; 1 g Dietary Fibre

Pictured on page 126.

Chocolate Banana Snack

Soft banana chunks with a firm coating of chocolate and toasted coconut. Kids enjoy making this treat as much as they enjoy making it disappear!

Milk chocolate candy bars (3 1/2 oz., 100 g, each), chopped	3	3
Medium bananas, cut into 1 inch (2.5 cm) slices	2	2
Flake coconut, toasted (see Tip, page 79)	1 1/2 cups	375 mL

Heat chocolate in medium saucepan on lowest heat for about 5 minutes, stirring often, until almost melted. Do not overheat. Remove from heat. Stir until smooth.

Dip banana into chocolate, allowing excess to drip back into saucepan.

Place coconut in shallow dish or on waxed paper. Roll banana in coconut to coat. Place on foil-lined baking sheet. Chill until set. Makes about 14 pieces.

1 piece: 178 Calories; 10.2 g Total Fat; 46 mg Sodium; 2 g Protein; 22 g Carbohydrate; 2 g Dietary Fibre

Pictured on page 72.

Hot Sauced Bananas

Sliced bananas topped with a golden sauce of orange, lemon and rum.
Serve with vanilla ice cream.

SAUCE		
Brown sugar, packed	1/2 cup	125 mL
All-purpose flour	2 tbsp.	30 mL
Prepared orange juice	1 cup	250 mL
Lemon juice	1 tbsp.	15 mL
Rum flavouring	1/2 tsp.	2 mL
Large bananas, sliced	2	2
Scoops of vanilla ice cream (optional)	4	4

Sauce: Stir brown sugar and flour in small saucepan.

Gradually stir in orange juice, lemon juice and flavouring. Heat and stir on medium-high for about 3 minutes until boiling and thickened. Makes 1 cup (250 mL) sauce.

Divide and put banana into 4 individual bowls. Divide ice cream among banana. Spoon sauce over top. Serves 4.

1 serving: 218 Calories; 0.4 g Total Fat; 13 mg Sodium; 2 g Protein; 55 g Carbohydrate; 2 g Dietary Fibre

Pictured on page 125.

1. Coconut Crunch Pudding, page 102
2. Hot Sauced Bananas, above
3. Frozen Cheesecake Bites, page 78

Props Courtesy Of: Wiltshire ®

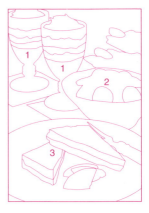

Snacks & Treats